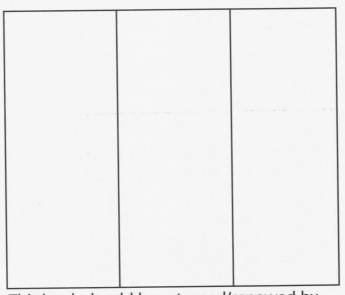

This book should be returned/renewed by
the latest date shown above. Overdue items
incur charges which prevent self-service
renewals. Please contact the library.

Wandsworth Libraries
24 hour Renewal Hotline
01159 293388
www.wandsworth.gov.uk

L.749A (2.07)

Wandsworth

PHILIP'S JUNIOR SCHOOL ATLAS

Philip's World Atlases are published in association with The Royal Geographical Society (with The Institute of British Geographers).

The Society was founded in 1830 and given a Royal Charter in 1859 for 'the advancement of geographical science'. Today it is a leading world centre for geographical learning – supporting education, teaching, research and expeditions, and promoting public understanding of the subject.

Further information about the Society and how to join may be found on its website at: www.rgs.org

Published in Great Britain by Philip's, a division of Octopus Publishing Group Limited, www.octopusbooks.co.uk
2–4 Heron Quays, London E14 4JP
An Hachette Livre UK Company
www.hachettelivre.co.uk

Cartography by Philip's

Ordnance Survey® Page 2 Bath city map (top right): This product includes mapping licensed from Ordnance Survey® with the permission of the Controller of Her Majesty's Stationery Office. © Crown copyright 2006. All rights reserved. Licence number 100011710.

© 1993, 2008 Philip's
First published 1993
Second edition 1997
Third edition 1999
Fourth edition 2003
Fifth edition 2006
Sixth edition 2008

A CIP catalogue record for this book is available from the British Library.

ISBN 978-0-540-09247-5 (HARDBACK EDITION)
ISBN 978-0-540-09248-2 (PAPERBACK EDITION)

Printed in Hong Kong

Details of other Philip's titles and services can be found on our website at: www.philips-maps.co.uk

What is a map?

These small maps explain the meaning of some of the lines and colours on the atlas maps.

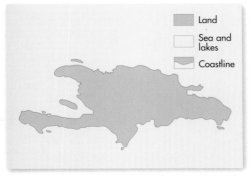

1. Land and sea This is how an island is shown on a map. The land is coloured green and the sea is blue. The coastline is a blue line.

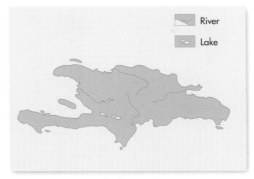

2. Rivers and lakes There are some lakes on the island and rivers that flow down to the sea.

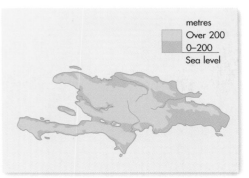

3. Height of the land – 1 This map shows the land over 200 metres high in a lighter colour. The height of the land is shown by contour lines and layer colours.

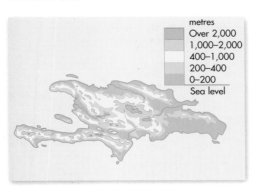

4. Height of the land – 2 This map shows more contour lines and layer colours. It shows that the highest land is in the centre of the island and that it is over 2,000 metres high.

5. Countries This is a way of showing different information about the island. It shows that the island is divided into two countries. They are separated by a country boundary.

6. Cities and towns There are cities and towns on the island. The two capital cities are shown with a special symbol. Other large or important cities are also shown by a red square or circle.

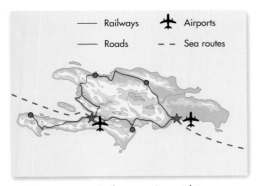

7. Transport information This map shows the most important roads, railways, airports and sea routes. Transport routes connect the cities and towns.

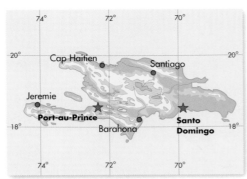

8. Where is the island? This map gives the lines of latitude and longitude and shows where the island is in the world. Page 59 in the atlas shows the same island at a different scale.

9. A complete map – using the country colouring and showing the letter-figure codes used in the index.

1

Scale

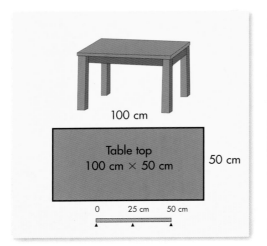

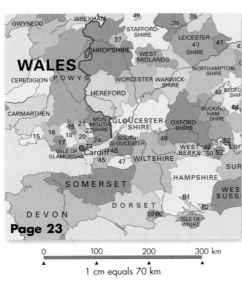

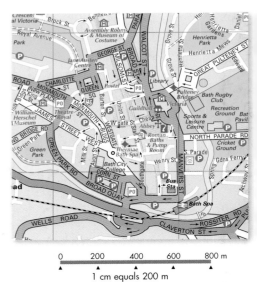

This is a drawing of the top of a table, looking down on it. It is 100 cm wide and 50 cm from front to back. The drawing measures 4 × 2 cm. It is drawn to scale: 1 cm on the drawing equals 25 cm on the table.

This is a plan of a room looking down from above. 1 cm on the map equals 1 metre in the room. The same table is shown, but now at a smaller scale. Use the scale bar to find the measurements of other parts of the room.

This is a map of an area in the city of Bath. Large buildings can be seen but other buildings are too small to show. Below are atlas maps of different scales.

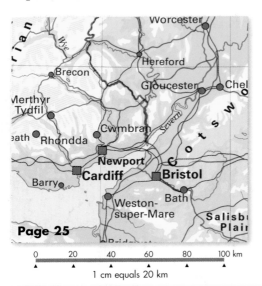

Page 25

0   20   40   60   80   100 km

1 cm equals 20 km

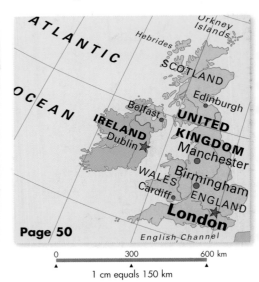

Page 23

0   100   200   300 km

1 cm equals 70 km

Page 50

0   300   600 km

1 cm equals 150 km

Scale bars

This distance represents 1 mile

This distance represents 1 kilometre

These examples of scale bars are at the scale of 1 cm equals 0.5 km

Signposts still have miles on them. 1 mile = 1.6 km, or 10 miles is the same as 16 kilometres. On maps of continents in this atlas, both a kilometre and a mile scale bar are shown.

On the maps of the continents, where you cannot see the British Isles, a small map of the British Isles is shown. It gives you some idea of size and scale.

BRITISH ISLES
On same scale

Direction

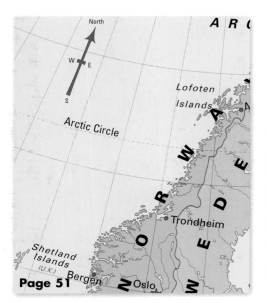

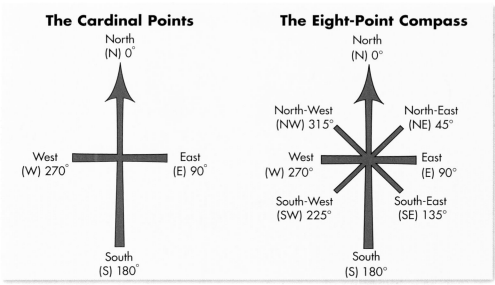

The Cardinal Points

The Eight-Point Compass

Many of the maps in this atlas have a North Point showing the direction of north. It points in the same direction as the lines of longitude. The four main directions shown are called the cardinal points.

Direction is measured in degrees. This diagram shows the degree numbers for each cardinal point. The direction is measured clockwise from north. The diagram on the right shows all the points of the compass and the divisions between the cardinal points. For example, between north and east there is north-east, between south and west is south-west. You can work out the cardinal points at your home by looking for the sun rising in the east and setting in the west.

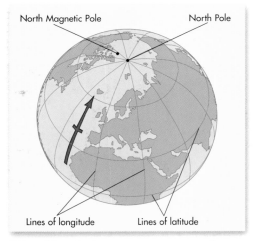

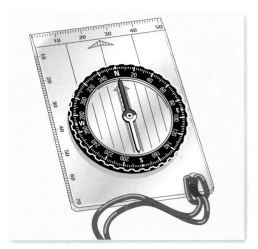

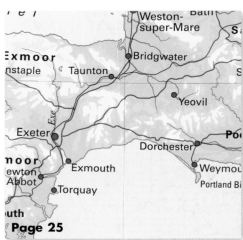

The Earth has a spot near the North Pole that is called the Magnetic Pole. If a piece of metal that was magnetized at one end was left to float, then the magnetized tip would point to the North Magnetic Pole.

The needle of a compass is magnetized and it always points north. If you know where you are and want to go to another place, you can measure your direction from a map and use a compass to guide you.

This is part of map 25. North is at the top. Look at the points of the compass on the diagram above and the positions of places on the map. Taunton is north-east of Exeter and Dorchester is south-east of Taunton.

3

Latitude and longitude

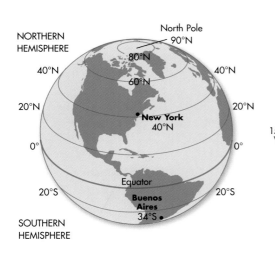

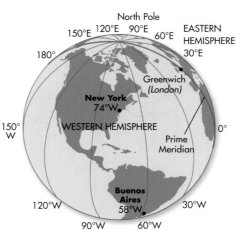

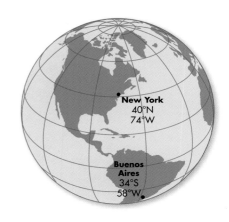

Latitude

This map shows part of the Earth seen from thousands of kilometres above New York. The Equator is exactly halfway between the North and South Poles. It divides the Earth into two hemispheres. The Equator is shown as a line on maps. It is numbered 0°. There are other lines on maps north and south of the Equator. They are called lines of latitude.

Longitude

Maps have another set of lines running north to south linking the Poles. These lines are called lines of longitude. The line numbered 0° runs through Greenwich in London, England, and is called the Prime Meridian. The other lines of longitude are numbered up to 180° east and west of 0°. Longitude line 180° runs through the Pacific Ocean.

Map references

The latitude and longitude lines on maps form a grid. In this atlas, the grid lines are in blue, and on most maps are shown for every ten degrees. The numbers of the lines can be used to give a reference to show the location of a place on a map. The index in this atlas uses another way of finding places. It lists the rows of latitude as numbers and the columns of longitude as letters.

Line of latitude with its number in degrees
Line of longitude with its number in degrees
Row number used in the index
Column letter used in the index

	Latitude	Longitude	Map page	Map letter-figure
Cairo, Africa	30°N	31°E	55	F2
Mexico City, N. America	19°N	99°W	59	H7
Mumbai, Asia	18°N	72°E	53	H7
Moscow, Europe	55°N	37°E	51	Q4
Sao Paulo, S. America	24°S	48°W	61	F6
Sydney, Oceania	34°S	151°E	57	F11

This table shows the largest city in each continent with its latitude and longitude. Look for them on the maps in this atlas.

Map information

Symbols

Page 17

△ A map symbol shows the position of something – for example, circles for towns or an aeroplane for an airport.

Page 37

△ On some maps a dot or a symbol stands for a large number – for example, ten million people or two million tonnes of wheat or potatoes.

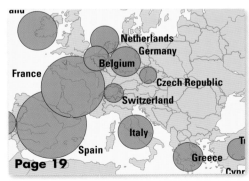

Page 19

△ The size of the symbol can be bigger or smaller, to show different numbers. The symbol here shows tourists.

Colours

Page 51

△ Colours are used on some maps so that separate areas, such as countries, as in this map, can be seen clearly.

Page 34

△ Patterns on maps often spread across country borders. This map shows different types of vegetation in the world.

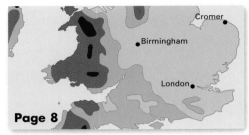

Page 8

△ On other maps, areas that are the same in some way have the same colour to show patterns. This map shows rainfall.

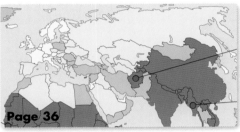

Page 36

△ Colours that are lighter or darker are used on some maps to show less or more of something. This map shows farming.

Graphs and charts

Graphs and charts are used to give more information about subjects shown on the maps. A graph shows how something changes over time.

This graph shows the rainfall for each month in a year as a blue bar that can be measured on the scale at the side of the graph.

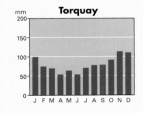

Page 8

This diagram is called a pie-chart. It shows how you can divide a total into its parts.

Page 15

This is a bar-chart. It is another way of showing a total divided into parts.

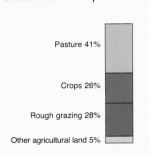

Page 13

Rocks, mountains and rivers

Rocks

This map shows the different types of rock in Great Britain and Ireland.

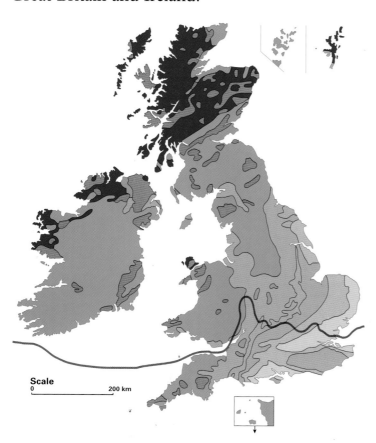

Scale
0 ———— 200 km

Type of rock

Younger rocks ↑

	Young sand, clay and river mud
	Chalk
	Sandstone, clay and young limestone
	The limestone part
	Old hard rocks, limestone, grit, coal, slate, shale and old sandstone
	Very old hard rocks

Older rocks

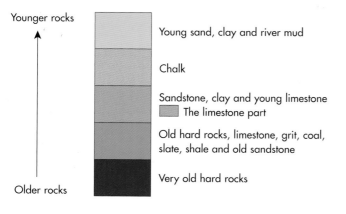

Old volcanoes, granite and basalt

——— Glaciers came as far south as this line up to 10,000 years ago

Longest rivers

(length in kilometres)

Shannon	370
Severn	354
Thames	335
Trent	297
Aire	259
Ouse	230
Wye	215
Tay	188
Nene	161
Clyde	158

Largest islands

(square kilometres)

Great Britain	229,880
Ireland	84,400
Lewis and Harris	2,225
Skye	1,666
Shetland (Mainland)	967
Mull	899
Anglesey	714
Islay	615
Isle of Man	572
Isle of Wight	381

Largest lakes

(square kilometres)

Lough Neagh	382
Lough Corrib	168
Lough Derg	120
Lower Lough Erne	105
Loch Lomond	71
Loch Ness	57

The largest lake in England is Lake Windermere (15 square kilometres). The largest lake in Wales is Lake Vyrnwy (8 square kilometres).

Highest mountains

(height in metres)

In Scotland:	
Ben Nevis	1,347
In Wales:	
Snowdon	1,085
In Ireland:	
Carrauntoohill	1,041
In England:	
Scafell Pike	978
In Northern Ireland:	
Slieve Donard	852

Scale
0 ———— 200 km

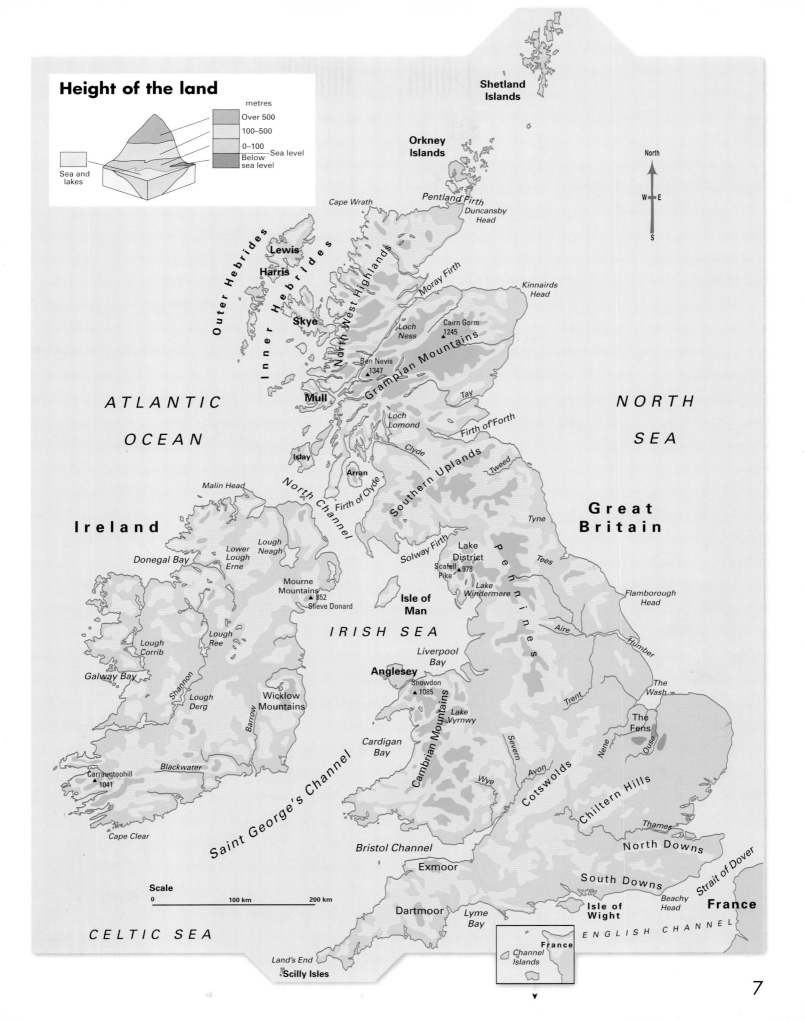

Height of the land

metres
Over 500
100–500
0–100
Sea level
Below sea level

Sea and lakes

North
W E
S

Shetland Islands

Orkney Islands

Cape Wrath
Pentland Firth
Duncansby Head

Outer Hebrides
Lewis
Harris

Inner Hebrides

North West Highlands

Moray Firth
Kinnairds Head

Skye

Loch Ness
Cairn Gorm
▲1245

Ben Nevis
▲1347

Grampian Mountains

Mull

Tay

A T L A N T I C

O C E A N

Loch Lomond

Firth of Forth

Islay

Clyde

Arran

Tweed

Southern Uplands

N O R T H

S E A

Malin Head

North Channel

Firth of Clyde

Ireland

Donegal Bay

Lower Lough Erne

Lough Neagh

Tyne

Great Britain

Solway Firth

Lake District
Scafell ▲978
Pike

Pennines

Tees

Lough Ree

Mourne Mountains
▲852
Sleve Donard

Isle of Man

Lake Windermere

Flamborough Head

Lough Corrib

Lough Derg

Wicklow Mountains

Barrow

Shannon

IRISH SEA

Liverpool Bay

Aire

Humber

Galway Bay

Anglesey

Snowdon
▲1085

Lake Vyrnwy

Trent

The Wash

Carrauntoohill
▲1041

Blackwater

Cambrian Mountains

The Fens

Nene
Ouse

Cardigan Bay

Severn

Avon

Cotswolds

Chiltern Hills

Saint George's Channel

Wye

Cape Clear

Bristol Channel

Exmoor

Thames

North Downs

South Downs

Beachy Head

Strait of Dover

France

Dartmoor

Lyme Bay

Isle of Wight

CELTIC SEA

Scale
0   100 km   200 km

Land's End

Scilly Isles

ENGLISH CHANNEL

France
Channel Islands

Weather and climate

Rainfall is measured at many places in the UK every day. Each year, all the measurements are put together and graphs are made, like the ones shown on this page. Experts in the weather use these measurements to find out the average amount of rainfall in the UK for each year. They can then show this on weather maps, like the map below. Graphs and maps are also made for average temperatures and other types of weather (see opposite page). These help the experts to see patterns in the UK's weather over a long period of time. These patterns in the weather show a country's climate. The maps on these pages show you the climate of Great Britain and Ireland.

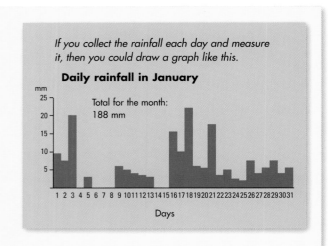

If you collect the rainfall each day and measure it, then you could draw a graph like this.

Daily rainfall in January

Total for the month: 188 mm

Rainfall

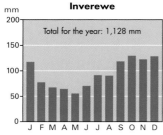

Inverewe

Total for the year: 1,128 mm

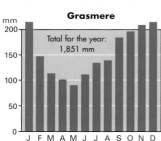

Grasmere

Total for the year: 1,851 mm

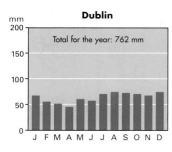

Dublin

Total for the year: 762 mm

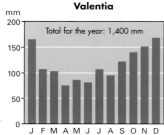

Valentia

Total for the year: 1,400 mm

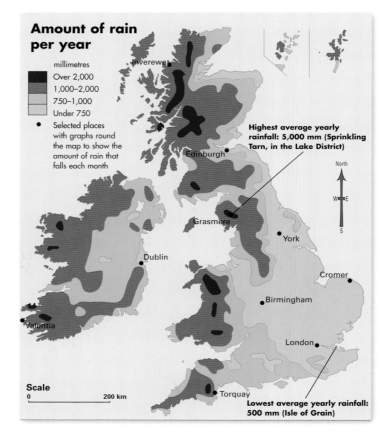

Amount of rain per year

millimetres
- Over 2,000
- 1,000–2,000
- 750–1,000
- Under 750

• Selected places with graphs round the map to show the amount of rain that falls each month

Highest average yearly rainfall: 5,000 mm (Sprinkling Tarn, in the Lake District)

Lowest average yearly rainfall: 500 mm (Isle of Grain)

North
West – East
South

Scale
0   200 km

Torquay

Total for the year: 950 mm

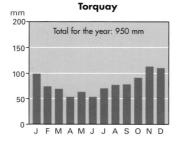

Birmingham

Total for the year: 764 mm

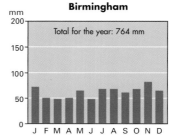

Edinburgh

Total for the year: 700 mm

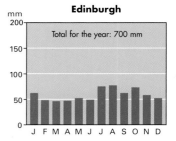

York

Total for the year: 639 mm

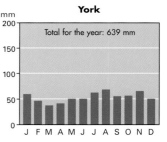

Cromer

Total for the year: 618 mm

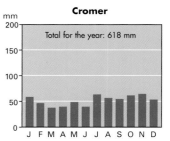

London

Total for the year: 593 mm

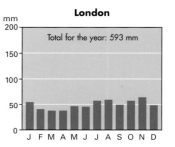

Wind

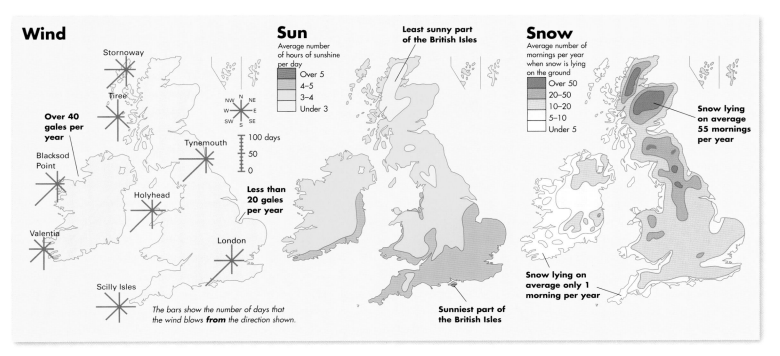

Stornoway

Tiree

Over 40 gales per year

Blacksod Point

Tynemouth

Holyhead

Valentia

London

Scilly Isles

Less than 20 gales per year

NW N NE
W E
SW S SE

100 days
50
0

*The bars show the number of days that the wind blows **from** the direction shown.*

Sun

Average number of hours of sunshine per day

Over 5
4–5
3–4
Under 3

Least sunny part of the British Isles

Sunniest part of the British Isles

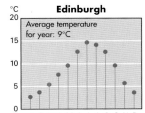

Snow

Average number of mornings per year when snow is lying on the ground

Over 50
20–50
10–20
5–10
Under 5

Snow lying on average 55 mornings per year

Snow lying on average only 1 morning per year

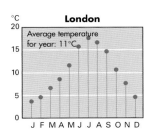

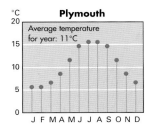

Temperature

Birmingham
°C
20
15
10
5
0
Average temperature for year: 10°C
J F M A M J J A S O N D

Dublin
°C
20
15
10
5
0
Average temperature for year: 10°C
J F M A M J J A S O N D

Edinburgh
°C
20
15
10
5
0
Average temperature for year: 9°C
J F M A M J J A S O N D

London
°C
20
15
10
5
0
Average temperature for year: 11°C
J F M A M J J A S O N D

Plymouth
°C
20
15
10
5
0
Average temperature for year: 11°C
J F M A M J J A S O N D

Winter temperature

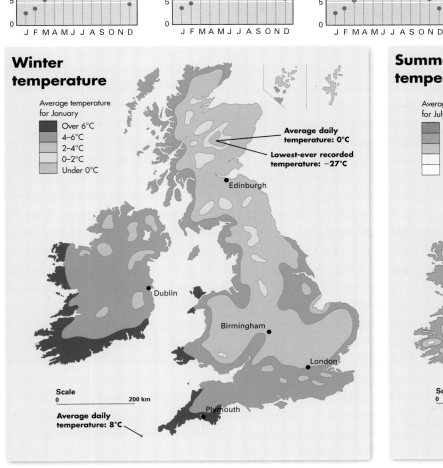

Average temperature for January

Over 6°C
4–6°C
2–4°C
0–2°C
Under 0°C

Average daily temperature: 0°C

Lowest-ever recorded temperature: −27°C

Edinburgh

Dublin

Birmingham

London

Scale
0   200 km

Average daily temperature: 8°C

Plymouth

Summer temperature

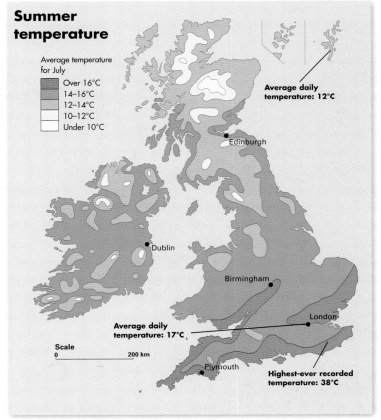

Average temperature for July

Over 16°C
14–16°C
12–14°C
10–12°C
Under 10°C

Average daily temperature: 12°C

Edinburgh

Dublin

Birmingham

London

Average daily temperature: 17°C

Scale
0   200 km

Plymouth

Highest-ever recorded temperature: 38°C

9

People, cities and towns

The UK Census

Every ten years, there is a government survey in the UK. The head of each household has to fill in a form. On the form, there are questions about the house and the people who live there. This is called the Census. The Census tells the government the number of people living in the UK. This helps the government to plan such things as schools and hospitals. The Census shows how the population has changed during the last century.

Here are some of the questions asked on the Census form:
How old are you?
Have you moved house in the last year?
In which country were you born?
To which ethnic group do you belong?
Have you a long-term illness?
Can you speak Welsh?
What do you do for a job?
How many hours a week do you work?
How do you get to work?
Where do you work?
Do you own or rent your house?
Do you have a bath, flush toilet or central heating?
Do you have a car?

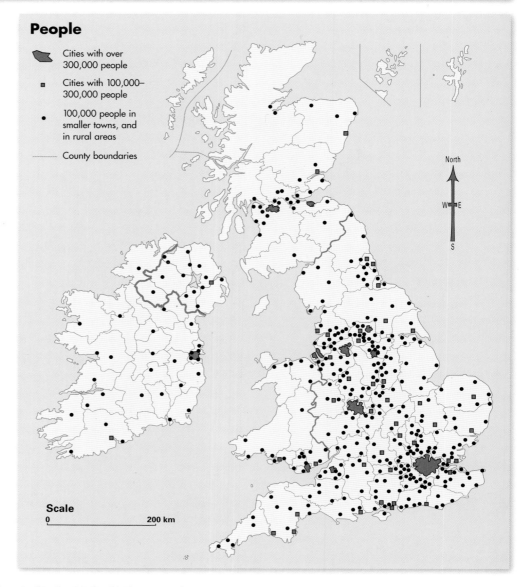

People

- Cities with over 300,000 people
- Cities with 100,000–300,000 people
- 100,000 people in smaller towns, and in rural areas
- County boundaries

North
W—E
S

Scale
0   200 km

Country population data

	1901	1951	2001
		millions	
England	30.5	41.2	49.2
Wales	2.0	2.6	2.9
Scotland	4.5	5.1	5.1
Northern Ireland	1.2	1.4	1.7
United Kingdom	**38.2**	**50.3**	**58.9**
Isle of Man	0.055	0.005	0.076
Channel Islands	0.096	0.102	0.147
Ireland	**3.2**	**2.9**	**3.9**

Changing numbers

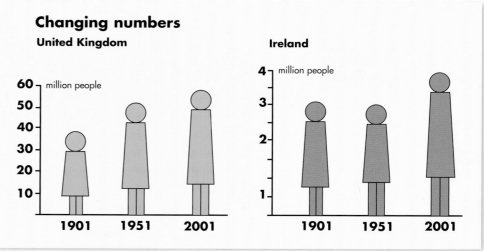

United Kingdom

million people

Ireland

million people

Cities

Cities with over 300,000 people

Cities with 100,000–300,000 people

Scale

0   200 km

Population in 1981, 1991 and 2001

	1981	1991	2001
		thousand people	
London	6,806	6,890	7,188
Birmingham	1,021	1,007	976
Leeds	718	717	716
Glasgow	774	689	579
Sheffield	548	529	513
Edinburgh	446	440	449
Liverpool	517	481	439
Manchester	463	439	393
Bristol	401	397	392
Cardiff	281	294	308
Leicester	283	285	287
Nottingham	278	281	284
Belfast	315	294	277
Newcastle	284	278	260
Hull	274	267	260
Plymouth	253	254	255
Stoke-on-Trent	252	253	254
Dublin	915	940	977
Cork	150	174	180

These are the largest cities in the UK and Ireland. Note that very few increased their populations between 1981 and 2001.

Young people

In these counties, young people are a large group in the population (over 20%). On this map young people are those aged under 15 years old.

In these counties, old people are a large group in the population (over 20%). On this map old people are women aged over 60 and men over 65 years old.

Look at these two maps. Can you think of some reasons why some counties have more older people than other counties?

Old people

11

Farming and fishing

Types of farm

Dairy farms
Cows for milk, butter and cheese

Beef farms
Cows and calves for beef and veal

Sheep farms
Sheep and lambs for wool and meat

Grain and root farms
Wheat, potatoes, sugar beet and oilseed rape

Mixed farms
Livestock and grain or roots

Market gardening
Vegetables, fruit and flowers

Forests

Big cities

The small maps show where different types of crops are grown.

North

W — E

S

Scale
0 — 200 km

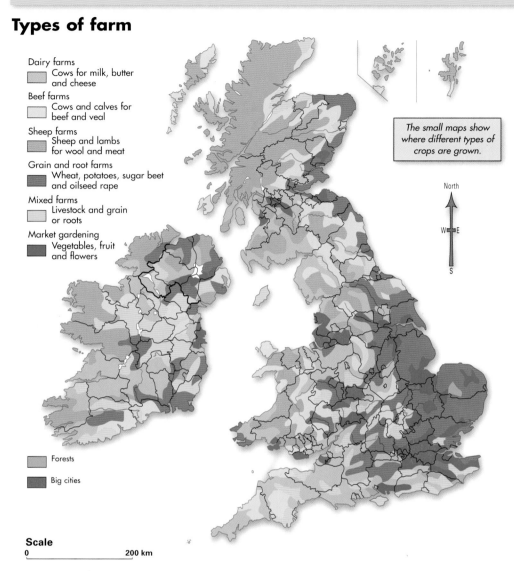

Wheat
square kilometres

Over 1,000

250–1,000 in each county

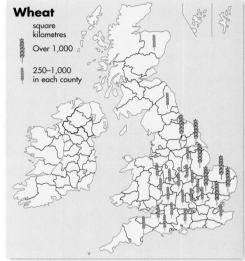

Potatoes
square kilometres

Over 100

25–100 in each county

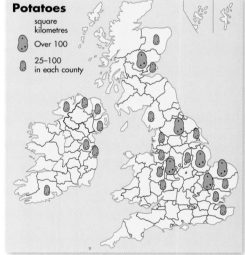

Oilseed rape
square kilometres

Over 200

50–200 in each county

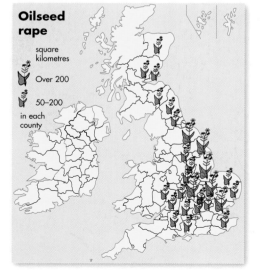

Sugar beet
square kilometres

Over 100

10–100 in each county

Vegetables
square kilometres

Over 100

10–100 in each county

Cattle

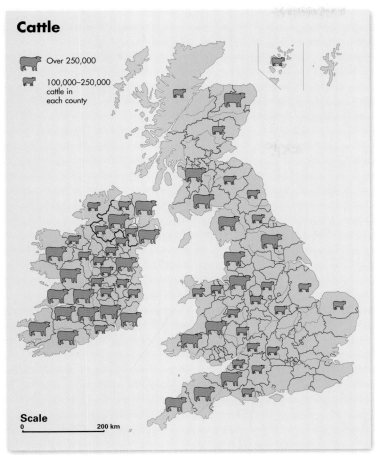

- Over 250,000
- 100,000–250,000 cattle in each county

Scale
0 — 200 km

Sheep and pigs

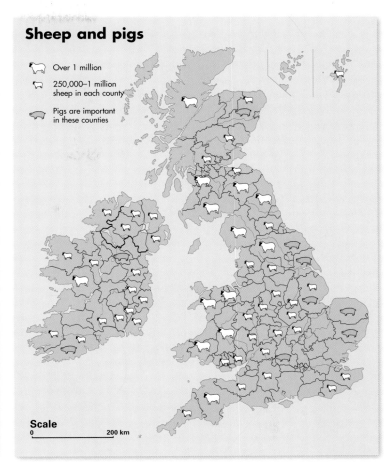

- Over 1 million
- 250,000–1 million sheep in each county
- Pigs are important in these counties

Scale
0 — 200 km

Land use in the UK

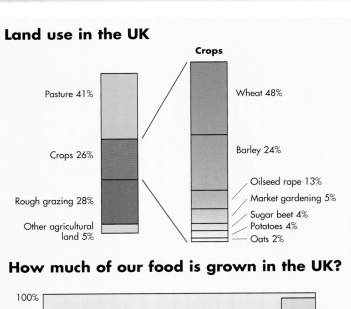

Crops

- Pasture 41%
- Crops 26%
- Rough grazing 28%
- Other agricultural land 5%

- Wheat 48%
- Barley 24%
- Oilseed rape 13%
- Market gardening 5%
- Sugar beet 4%
- Potatoes 4%
- Oats 2%

How much of our food is grown in the UK?

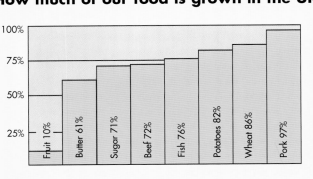

- Fruit 10%
- Butter 61%
- Sugar 71%
- Beef 72%
- Fish 76%
- Potatoes 82%
- Wheat 86%
- Pork 97%

Fishing

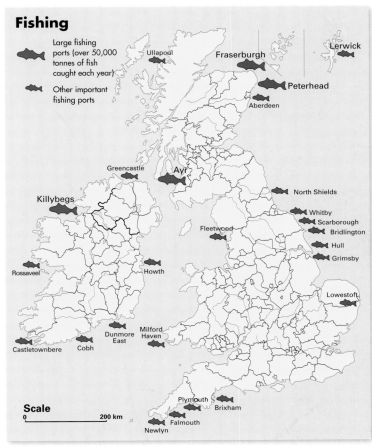

- Large fishing ports (over 50,000 tonnes of fish caught each year)
- Other important fishing ports

Ullapool, Fraserburgh, Lerwick, Peterhead, Aberdeen, Greencastle, Ayr, North Shields, Killybegs, Whitby, Scarborough, Bridlington, Fleetwood, Hull, Grimsby, Rossaveel, Howth, Lowestoft, Dunmore East, Milford Haven, Castletownbere, Cobh, Plymouth, Brixham, Falmouth, Newlyn

Scale
0 — 200 km

13

Work, industry and energy

Total employment
The number of
people working

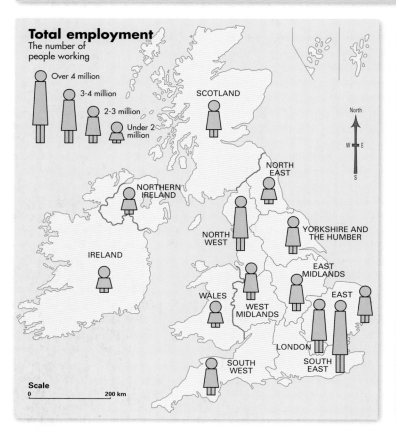

- Over 4 million
- 3-4 million
- 2-3 million
- Under 2 million

SCOTLAND

NORTHERN IRELAND

IRELAND

NORTH EAST

NORTH WEST

YORKSHIRE AND THE HUMBER

EAST MIDLANDS

WALES

WEST MIDLANDS

EAST

LONDON

SOUTH WEST

SOUTH EAST

Scale
0   200 km

North
W — E
S

Employment in services

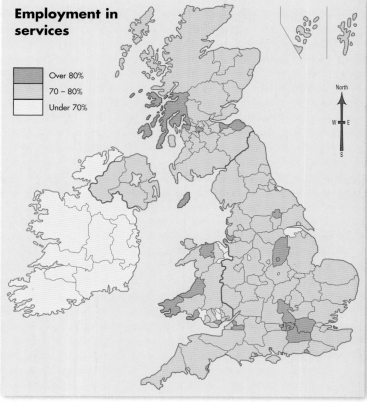

- Over 80%
- 70 – 80%
- Under 70%

North
W — E
S

Manufacturing industries are industries which make things. Some examples of manufactured goods are cars, steel, textiles and clothes.

Service industries do not make things. They provide a service to people. Shops, hotels and banks are examples of service industries.

Unemployment
% of the workforce who are unemployed

- 5 – 6%
- Over 6%

Employment in manufacturing
% of the workforce who are employed in manufacturing

- 15 – 20%
- Over 20%

Employment in agriculture
% of the workforce who are employed in agriculture, forestry and fishing

- 2.5 – 10%
- Over 10%

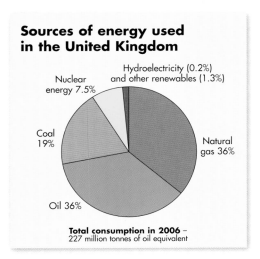

Sources of energy used in the United Kingdom

Hydroelectricity (0.2%) and other renewables (1.3%)

Nuclear energy 7.5%

Coal 19%

Natural gas 36%

Oil 36%

Total consumption in 2006 –
227 million tonnes of oil equivalent

Electricity generation in the United Kingdom (1980–2005)

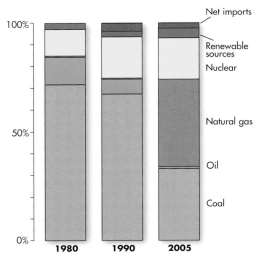

Net imports

Renewable sources

Nuclear

Natural gas

Oil

Coal

100%

50%

0%

1980 **1990** **2005**

This bar-chart shows the different types of fuel that are used to make electricity in the UK. The use of coal and oil in the generation of electricity has dropped over the 25-year period from 1980 to 2005. However, the use of natural gas has increased by 40%.

Renewable energy

Renewable sources used to generate electricity (in million tonnes of oil equivalent)

	1998	2002	2006
Biofuels	0.9	1.8	3.2
Hydroelectricity	0.4	0.4	0.4
Wind Power	0.1	0.1	0.4
Total renewable energy	1.4	2.3	4.0

In 2006 4.5% of electricity in the UK was generated by renewable energy sources. The government aims to increase this to 10% by 2010 and 20% by 2020.

Energy sources in Great Britain and Ireland

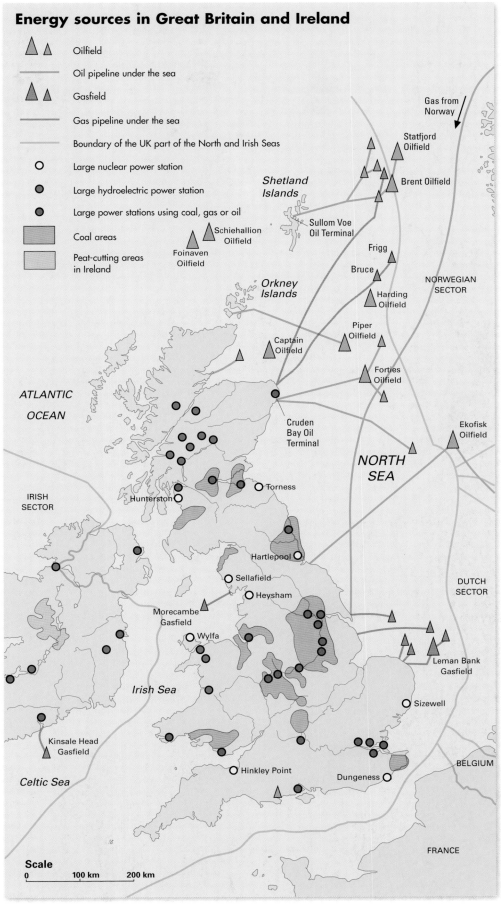

Oilfield

Oil pipeline under the sea

Gasfield

Gas pipeline under the sea

Boundary of the UK part of the North and Irish Seas

Large nuclear power station

Large hydroelectric power station

Large power stations using coal, gas or oil

Coal areas

Peat-cutting areas in Ireland

Gas from Norway

Statfjord Oilfield

Brent Oilfield

Shetland Islands

Sullom Voe Oil Terminal

Schiehallion Oilfield

Foinaven Oilfield

Frigg

Bruce

NORWEGIAN SECTOR

Harding Oilfield

Orkney Islands

Piper Oilfield

Captain Oilfield

Forties Oilfield

ATLANTIC OCEAN

Cruden Bay Oil Terminal

Ekofisk Oilfield

NORTH SEA

IRISH SECTOR

Torness

Hunterston

DUTCH SECTOR

Hartlepool

Sellafield

Heysham

Morecambe Gasfield

Wylfa

Leman Bank Gasfield

Irish Sea

Sizewell

Kinsale Head Gasfield

BELGIUM

Celtic Sea

Hinkley Point

Dungeness

FRANCE

Scale

0   100 km   200 km

Transport

There are about 380 thousand kilometres of road in the UK. The total number of cars, buses, lorries and motorbikes is 26 million. That is almost half the number of people in the UK. The maps on this page show the motorways and some main roads in the UK and the number of cars in the different regions. At the bottom of the page there are tables showing the road distances between important towns.

Cars

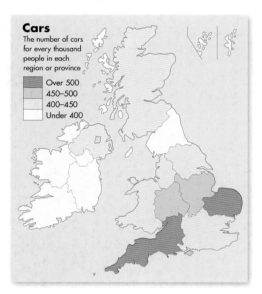

The number of cars for every thousand people in each region or province

- Over 500
- 450–500
- 400–450
- Under 400

Roads

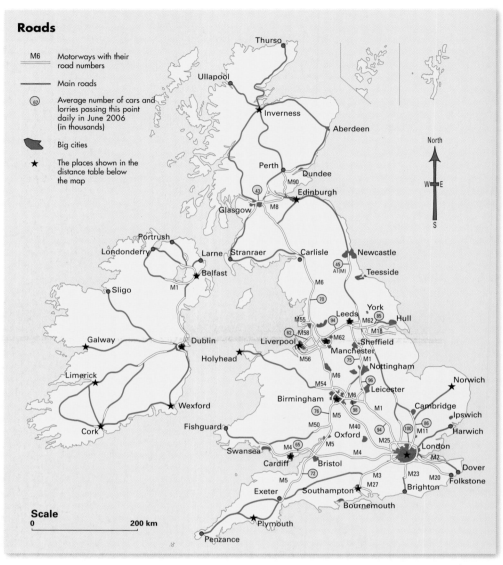

M6	Motorways with their road numbers
——	Main roads
(67)	Average number of cars and lorries passing this point daily in June 2006 (in thousands)
▰	Big cities
★	The places shown in the distance table below the map

Scale
0 — 200 km

Road distances

The distance tables are in kilometres, but distances on road signposts in the UK are in miles.
A mile is longer than a kilometre.
1 mile = 1.6 kilometres. 1 kilometre = 0.6 mile.

UK	Birmingham	Cardiff	Edinburgh	Holyhead	Inverness	Leeds	Liverpool	London	Manchester	Norwich	Plymouth	Southampton
Birmingham		163	460	246	716	179	151	179	130	249	320	206
Cardiff	163		587	341	843	341	264	249	277	381	259	192
Edinburgh	460	587		489	256	320	338	608	336	586	790	669
Holyhead	246	341	489		745	262	151	420	198	481	528	455
Inverness	716	843	256	745		579	605	864	604	842	1049	925
Leeds	179	341	320	262	579		119	306	64	277	502	378
Liverpool	151	264	338	151	605	119		330	55	360	452	357
London	179	249	608	420	864	306	330		309	172	343	127
Manchester	130	277	336	198	604	64	55	309		306	457	325
Norwich	249	381	586	481	842	277	360	172	306		515	299
Plymouth	320	259	790	528	1049	502	452	343	457	515		246
Southampton	206	192	669	455	925	378	357	127	325	299	246	

Ireland

	Belfast	Cork	Dublin	Galway	Limerick	Wexford
Belfast		418	160	300	222	306
Cork	418		257	193	97	190
Dublin	160	257		210	193	137
Galway	300	193	210		97	249
Limerick	222	97	193	97		193
Wexford	306	190	137	249	193	

Railways

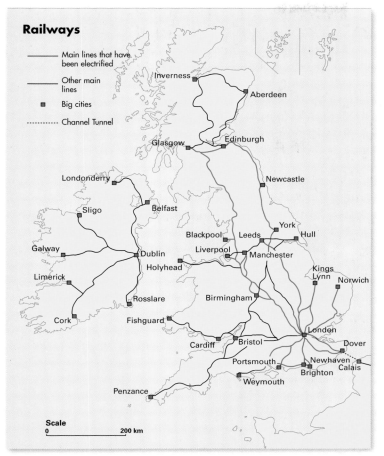

- ▬▬▬ Main lines that have been electrified
- ▬▬▬ Other main lines
- ■ Big cities
- ········ Channel Tunnel

Inverness
Aberdeen
Glasgow
Edinburgh
Londonderry
Sligo
Belfast
Newcastle
Galway
Dublin
Blackpool
Leeds
York
Hull
Liverpool
Holyhead
Manchester
Limerick
Kings Lynn
Norwich
Rosslare
Birmingham
Cork
Fishguard
London
Dover
Cardiff
Bristol
Portsmouth
Newhaven
Calais
Weymouth
Brighton
Penzance

Scale
0   200 km

Manchester – the daily flow of people

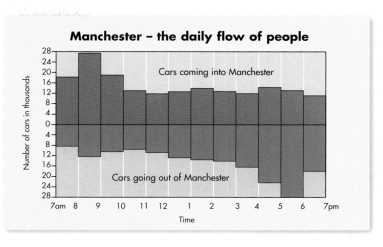

Cars coming into Manchester

Cars going out of Manchester

Number of cars in thousands

7am 8 9 10 11 12 1 2 3 4 5 6 7pm

Time

High speed rail

Edinburgh
Glasgow
Channel Tunnel
Cardiff
London
Ashford
Amsterdam
Hamburg
Brussels
Berlin
Rennes
Lille
Frankfurt
Paris
Munich
Berne
Bordeaux
Lyons
Bilbao
Milan
Marseilles
Madrid
Barcelona
Naples

By the year 2010 trains will be able to travel at over 200km/h on those lines shown on the map.

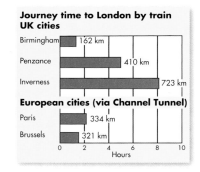

Journey time to London by train
UK cities

- Birmingham — 162 km
- Penzance — 410 km
- Inverness — 723 km

European cities (via Channel Tunnel)

- Paris — 334 km
- Brussels — 321 km

0   2   4   6   8   10
Hours

Ports and ferries

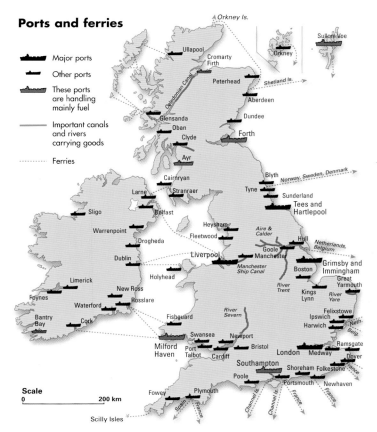

- 🚢 Major ports
- ⛴ Other ports
- ⛴ These ports are handling mainly fuel
- ▬▬ Important canals and rivers carrying goods
- ········ Ferries

Orkney Is.
Sullom Voe
Ullapool
Cromarty Firth
Orkney
Peterhead
Shetland Is.
Caledonian Canal
Aberdeen
Glensanda
Dundee
Oban
Clyde
Forth
Ayr
Cairnryan
Blyth
Larne
Tyne
Norway, Sweden, Denmark
Stranraer
Sunderland
Sligo
Belfast
Tees and Hartlepool
Warrenpoint
Heysham
Aire & Calder
Drogheda
Fleetwood
Hull
Dublin
Liverpool
Goole
Netherlands, Belgium
Limerick
Holyhead
Manchester
Manchester Ship Canal
Boston
Grimsby and Immingham
New Ross
River Trent
Kings Lynn
Great Yarmouth
Foynes
River Yare
Waterford
Rosslare
Felixstowe
Bantry Bay
Cork
Fishguard
River Severn
Ipswich
Harwich
Neth. Belg.
Swansea
Newport
Ramsgate
Milford Haven
Port Talbot
Cardiff
Bristol
London
Medway
France
Dover
Southampton
Shoreham
Folkestone
Poole
Portsmouth
Newhaven
Fowey
Plymouth
Channel Is.
France
Scilly Isles
Spain
France

Scale
0   200 km

Airports

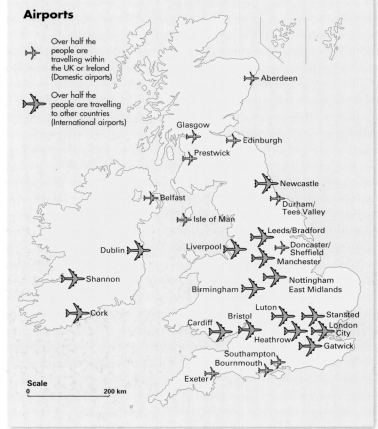

- ✈ Over half the people are travelling within the UK or Ireland (Domestic airports)
- ✈ Over half the people are travelling to other countries (International airports)

Aberdeen
Glasgow
Edinburgh
Prestwick
Newcastle
Belfast
Durham/Tees Valley
Isle of Man
Leeds/Bradford
Dublin
Liverpool
Doncaster/Sheffield
Manchester
Shannon
Birmingham
Nottingham East Midlands
Cork
Luton
Bristol
Stansted
Cardiff
London City
Heathrow
Gatwick
Southampton
Bournemouth
Exeter

Scale
0   200 km

Conservation and tourism

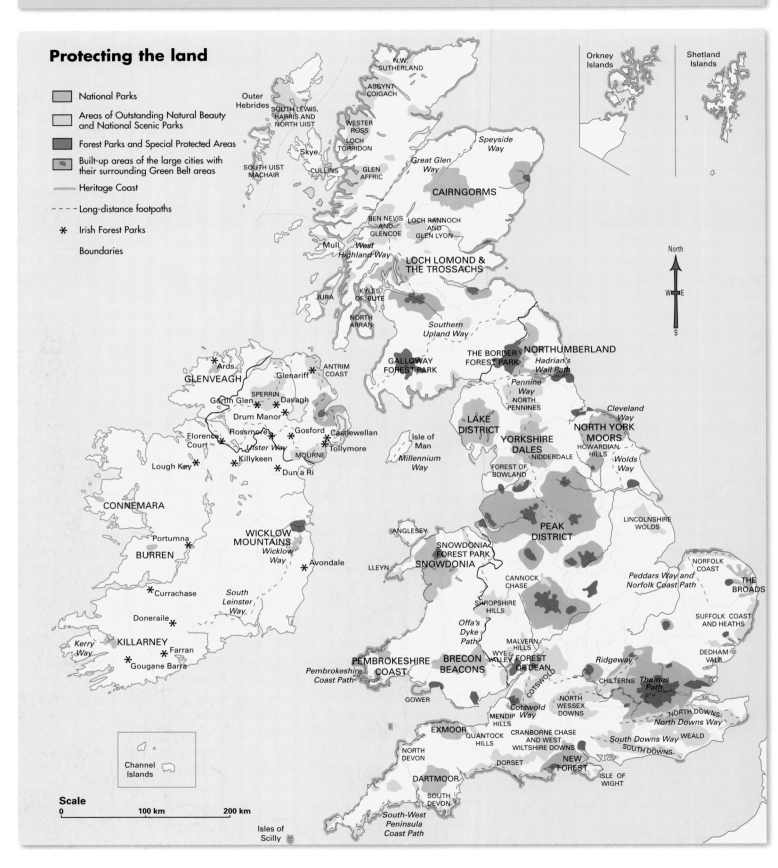

Protecting the land

Legend:
- National Parks
- Areas of Outstanding Natural Beauty and National Scenic Parks
- Forest Parks and Special Protected Areas
- Built-up areas of the large cities with their surrounding Green Belt areas
- Heritage Coast
- Long-distance footpaths
- * Irish Forest Parks
- Boundaries

Orkney Islands

Shetland Islands

N.W. SUTHERLAND

ASSYNT COIGACH

Outer Hebrides

SOUTH LEWIS, HARRIS AND NORTH UIST

WESTER ROSS

LOCH TORRIDON

Skye

Speyside Way

Great Glen Way

SOUTH UIST MACHAIR

CULLINS

GLEN AFFRIC

CAIRNGORMS

BEN NEVIS AND GLENCOE

LOCH RANNOCH AND GLEN LYON

Mull

West Highland Way

LOCH LOMOND & THE TROSSACHS

North

JURA

KYLES OF BUTE

NORTH ARRAN

Southern Upland Way

Ards

GLENVEAGH

Glenariff

ANTRIM COAST

GALLOWAY FOREST PARK

THE BORDER FOREST PARK

NORTHUMBERLAND

Hadrian's Wall Path

Gortin Glen

SPERRIN

Davagh

Pennine Way

NORTH PENNINES

Cleveland Way

Drum Manor

Florence Court

Rossmore

Gosford

Castlewellan

LAKE DISTRICT

YORKSHIRE DALES

NORTH YORK MOORS

HOWARDIAN HILLS

Wolds Way

Ulster Way

MOURNE

Tollymore

Isle of Man

Millennium Way

NIDDERDALE

Lough Key

Killykeen

Dun a Ri

FOREST OF BOWLAND

CONNEMARA

Portumna

BURREN

WICKLOW MOUNTAINS

Wicklow Way

Avondale

ANGLESEY

PEAK DISTRICT

LINCOLNSHIRE WOLDS

Currachase

South Leinster Way

LLEYN

SNOWDONIA FOREST PARK

SNOWDONIA

CANNOCK CHASE

NORFOLK COAST

Peddars Way and Norfolk Coast Path

THE BROADS

Doneraile

SHROPSHIRE HILLS

SUFFOLK COAST AND HEATHS

Kerry Way

KILLARNEY

Farran

Gougane Barra

Offa's Dyke Path

MALVERN HILLS

WYE VALLEY

FOREST OF DEAN

Ridgeway

CHILTERNS

Thames Path

DEDHAM VALE

Pembrokeshire Coast Path

PEMBROKESHIRE COAST

BRECON BEACONS

COTSWOLD

NORTH WESSEX DOWNS

NORTH DOWNS

North Downs Way

GOWER

Cotswold Way

MENDIP HILLS

CRANBORNE CHASE AND WEST WILTSHIRE DOWNS

South Downs Way

WEALD

SOUTH DOWNS

EXMOOR

QUANTOCK HILLS

NORTH DEVON

DORSET

NEW FOREST

ISLE OF WIGHT

DARTMOOR

SOUTH DEVON

South-West Peninsula Coast Path

Channel Islands

Scale

0   100 km   200 km

Isles of Scilly

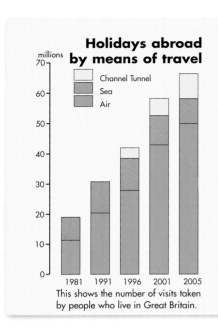

Holidays abroad by means of travel

millions

Channel Tunnel
Sea
Air

This shows the number of visits taken by people who live in Great Britain.

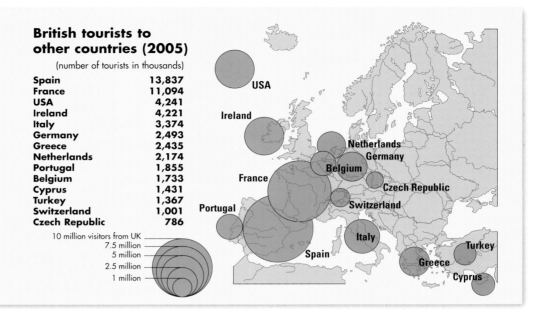

British tourists to other countries (2005)

(number of tourists in thousands)

Spain	13,837
France	11,094
USA	4,241
Ireland	4,221
Italy	3,374
Germany	2,493
Greece	2,435
Netherlands	2,174
Portugal	1,855
Belgium	1,733
Cyprus	1,431
Turkey	1,367
Switzerland	1,001
Czech Republic	786

10 million visitors from UK
7.5 million
5 million
2.5 million
1 million

Tourism

● Main holiday cities and towns
● Major tourist attractions

Scale
0   200 km

Visitors from other countries (2005)

(number of visitors in thousands)

USA	3,438
France	3,324
Germany	3,294
Ireland	2,806
Spain	1,786
Netherlands	1,720
Italy	1,186
Belgium	1,112
Australia	919
Canada	796
Sweden	728
Switzerland	699
Norway	627

Tourist attractions (2006)

(number of visitors in millions)

Blackpool Pleasure Beach	5.7
Tate Modern, London	4.9
British Museum, London	4.8
National Gallery, London	4.6
British Airways London Eye	4.1
Natural History Museum, London	3.8
River Lee Country Park, Hertfordshire	3.5
Xscape, Castleford	3.5
Science Museum, London	2.4
Victoria and Albert Museum, London	2.4
Tower of London	2.1
St Paul's Cathedral, London	1.6
Natural Portrait Gallery, London	1.6
Tate Britain, London	1.6
Great Yarmouth Pleasure Beach	1.4
Flamingo Land, Kirby Misperton	1.3
New Metroland, Gateshead	1.3
Lake Windermere	1.3
Kew Gardens, London	1.2
Chester Zoo	1.2

Water

Rainfall areas – wet and dry

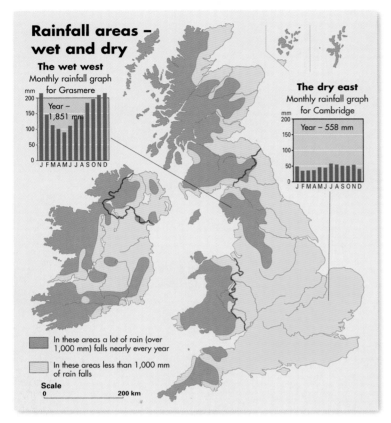

The wet west
Monthly rainfall graph for Grasmere

Year – 1,851 mm

mm
200
150
100
50
0
J F M A M J J A S O N D

The dry east
Monthly rainfall graph for Cambridge

Year – 558 mm

mm
200
150
100
50
0
J F M A M J J A S O N D

In these areas a lot of rain (over 1,000 mm) falls nearly every year

In these areas less than 1,000 mm of rain falls

Scale
0   200 km

Reservoirs and boreholes

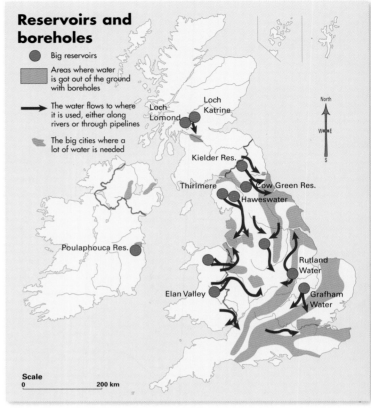

- Big reservoirs
- Areas where water is got out of the ground with boreholes
- → The water flows to where it is used, either along rivers or through pipelines
- The big cities where a lot of water is needed

North
W—E
S

Loch Lomond
Loch Katrine
Kielder Res.
Thirlmere
Cow Green Res.
Haweswater
Poulaphouca Res.
Rutland Water
Elan Valley
Grafham Water

Scale
0   200 km

Sources of river pollution

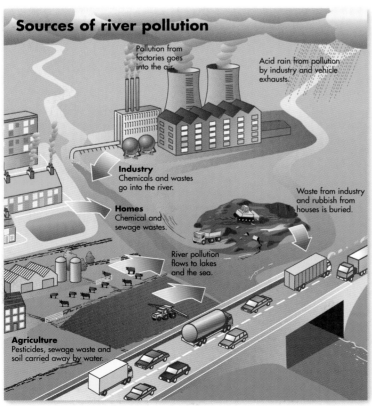

Pollution from factories goes into the air.

Acid rain from pollution by industry and vehicle exhausts.

Industry
Chemicals and wastes go into the river.

Homes
Chemical and sewage wastes.

Waste from industry and rubbish from houses is buried.

River pollution flows to lakes and the sea.

Agriculture
Pesticides, sewage waste and soil carried away by water.

River pollution

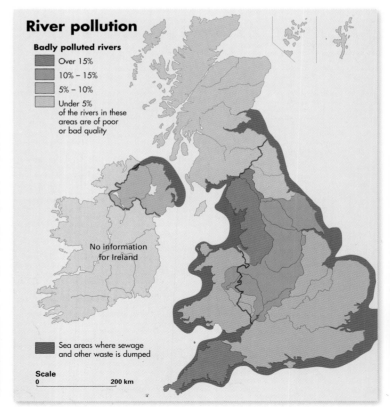

Badly polluted rivers
- Over 15%
- 10% – 15%
- 5% – 10%
- Under 5% of the rivers in these areas are of poor or bad quality

No information for Ireland

Sea areas where sewage and other waste is dumped

Scale
0   200 km

The average UK household uses 355 litres of water a day. Up to 135,000 million litres of water are used each day in the UK. Over half the water is used by people in their homes. About a third is used to make electricity. The rest is used in farms and factories. On the right are some of the ways that water is used in the home:

To make one car can use up to 30,000 litres of water. To brew one pint of beer needs 8 pints of water.

Domestic appliances – water usage

	(per wash)
Washing machine	80 litres
Bath	80 litres
Dishwasher	35 litres
Shower	35 litres
Toilet flush	6 litres

The water cycle

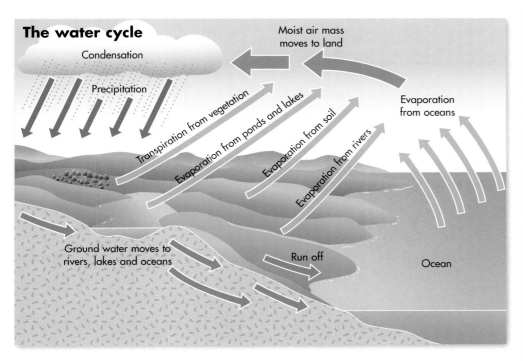

Domestic water and sewage (the man-made water cycle)

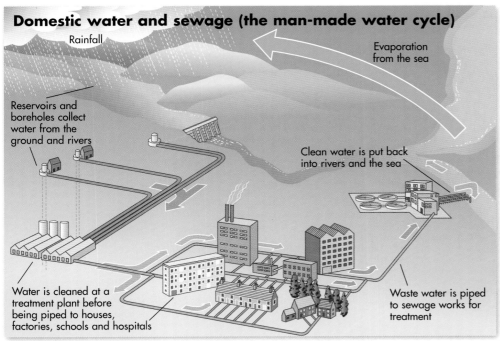

Flooding

Around 5 million people, in 2 million properties, live in flood risk areas in England and Wales. In summer 2007 there were several periods of extreme rainfall which led to widespread flooding.

The Environment Agency has an important role in warning people about the risk of flooding, and in reducing the likelihood of flooding from rivers and the sea.

Flood risk in England and Wales

▬ Areas at greatest risk from flooding

◊ Counties worst affected by flooding in summer 2007

Counties and regions

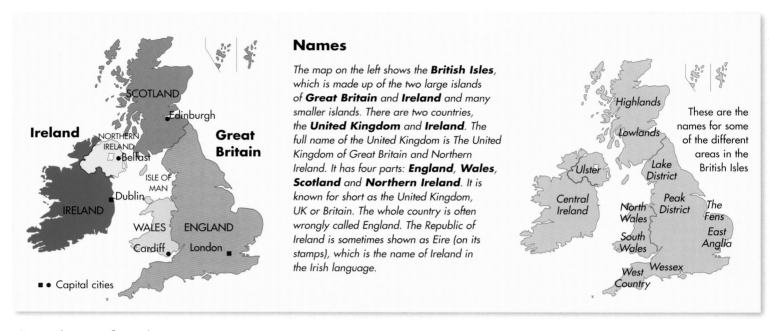

Names

The map on the left shows the **British Isles**, which is made up of the two large islands of **Great Britain** and **Ireland** and many smaller islands. There are two countries, the **United Kingdom** and **Ireland**. The full name of the United Kingdom is The United Kingdom of Great Britain and Northern Ireland. It has four parts: **England**, **Wales**, **Scotland** and **Northern Ireland**. It is known for short as the United Kingdom, UK or Britain. The whole country is often wrongly called England. The Republic of Ireland is sometimes shown as Eire (on its stamps), which is the name of Ireland in the Irish language.

These are the names for some of the different areas in the British Isles

Counties and regions

The map shows the Standard Regions of the United Kingdom. The boundaries follow those of the counties shown on page 23. Large bodies like the Health Service, Water or Electricity divide the country up into their own regions. Ireland is divided into four historic provinces.

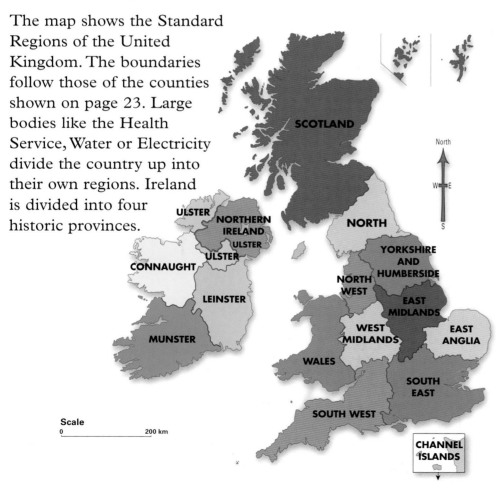

Counties and unitary authorities

England and Wales are divided into counties, unitary authorities and boroughs. The counties are divided into districts, and the districts into parishes and wards. Scotland is divided into regions and unitary authorities, and Northern Ireland into districts.

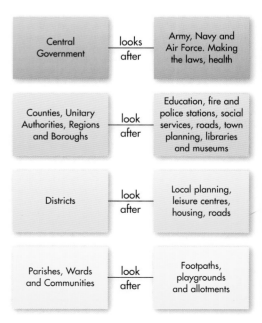

Central Government	looks after	Army, Navy and Air Force. Making the laws, health
Counties, Unitary Authorities, Regions and Boroughs	look after	Education, fire and police stations, social services, roads, town planning, libraries and museums
Districts	look after	Local planning, leisure centres, housing, roads
Parishes, Wards and Communities	look after	Footpaths, playgrounds and allotments

Area data

	Area in square kilometres
England	130,439
Wales	20,768
Scotland	77,167
Northern Ireland	13,483
United Kingdom	**241,857**
Isle of Man	**572**
Channel Islands	**195**
Ireland	**68,896**

The Channel Islands and the Isle of Man are dependencies of the Crown and have their own parliaments. They are not part of the United Kingdom.

The six counties are shown in Northern Ireland. It is divided for local government into 26 districts.
The map shows the 6 counties in Northern Ireland, the 32 unitary authorities in Scotland, the 22 unitary authorities in Wales, and the 87 unitary authorities in England as of 1 April 1998. Authorities which are too small to name on the map are numbered and listed separately.

SCOTLAND
1. ABERDEEN CITY
2. DUNDEE CITY
3. WEST DUNBARTONSHIRE
4. EAST DUNBARTONSHIRE
5. CITY OF GLASGOW
6. INVERCLYDE
7. RENFREWSHIRE
8. EAST RENFREWSHIRE
9. NORTH LANARKSHIRE
10. FALKIRK
11. CLACKMANNANSHIRE
12. WEST LOTHIAN
13. CITY OF EDINBURGH
14. MIDLOTHIAN

WALES
15. SWANSEA
16. NEATH PORT TALBOT
17. BRIDGEND
18. RHONDDA CYNON TAFF
19. MERTHYR TYDFIL
20. CAERPHILLY
21. BLAENAU GWENT
22. TORFAEN
23. CARDIFF
24. NEWPORT

ENGLAND
25. HARTLEPOOL
26. DARLINGTON
27. STOCKTON-ON-TEES
28. MIDDLESBROUGH
29. REDCAR AND CLEVELAND
30. BLACKPOOL
31. BLACKBURN WITH DARWEN
32. HALTON
33. WARRINGTON
34. KINGSTON UPON HULL
35. NORTH EAST LINCOLNSHIRE
36. STOKE-ON-TRENT
37. TELFORD AND WREKIN
38. DERBY CITY
39. CITY OF NOTTINGHAM
40. LEICESTER CITY
41. RUTLAND
42. PETERBOROUGH
43. MILTON KEYNES
44. LUTON
45. NORTH SOMERSET
46. CITY OF BRISTOL
47. BATH AND N. E. SOMERSET
48. SWINDON
49. READING
50. WOKINGHAM
51. WINDSOR AND MAIDENHEAD
52. SLOUGH
53. BRACKNELL FOREST
54. THURROCK
55. SOUTHEND-ON-SEA
56. MEDWAY
57. PLYMOUTH
58. TORBAY
59. POOLE
60. BOURNEMOUTH
61. SOUTHAMPTON
62. PORTSMOUTH
63. BRIGHTON AND HOVE

● Capital cities

Scale

0   100 km   200 km

England and Wales

24

Map information

Height of land

metres	
Over 1000	
400–1000	
200–400	
100–200	
0–100	
Below sea level	
Sea	

▲ 978 Highest point

Rivers
Main roads
Main railways
✈ Main airports
● Cities and towns
★ Capital city
Country boundaries
Lines of latitude and longitude

1 Index squares – see index

MAP SCALE
This distance is 100 kilometres
This distance is 50 miles

NORTH SEA

IRISH SEA

North Channel

SCOTLAND

NORTHERN IRELAND

Belfast

Bangor
Larne

Stranraer
Mull of Galloway

Campbeltown
Kintyre
Jura
Arran
Isle of Man
Snaefell 620 ▲
Douglas

Girvan
Ayr
Irvine
Kilmarnock
East Kilbride
Paisley
Greenock
Dumbarton
Clydebank
Glasgow
Hamilton
Stirling
Falkirk
Kirkcaldy
Dunfermline
Glenrothes
Edinburgh
Firth of Forth
Dunbar
Berwick-upon-Tweed
Galashiels
Jedburgh
Hawick
Cheviot Hills
Alnwick
Newcastle-upon-Tyne
Tynemouth
South Shield
Sunderland
Gateshead
Hartlepool
Redcar
Middlesbrough
Whitby
Scarborough
Bridlington

Southern Uplands
Dumfries
Carlisle
Hadrian's Wall
Penrith
Solway Firth
Workington
Whitehaven
Lake District
Cumbrian Mountains
Scafell Pike 978 ▲
Barrow-in-Furness
Morecambe Bay
Lancaster
Preston
Blackpool

Pennines
Durham
Wear
Tees
Darlington
North York Moors
York
Yorkshire Wolds
Harrogate
Skipton
Keighley
Bradford
Leeds
Huddersfield
Halifax
Burnley
Blackburn
Ribble
Oldham
Manchester
Stockport
Bolton
Warrington
Liverpool
Birkenhead
Mersey
Chester
Crewe
Newcastle-under-Lyme
Stoke-on-Trent
Wrexham

Kingston upon Hull
Grimsby
Humber
Lincolnshire Wolds
Louth
Skegness
The Wash
King's Lynn
Norwich
Cromer
Boston
Grantham
Newark
Lincoln
Doncaster
Rotherham
Sheffield
Chesterfield
Mansfield
Nottingham
Trent
Derby
Ouse

Llandudno
Bangor
Anglesey
Holyhead
Caernarfon
Snowdon 1085
Pwllheli

Stafford
Severn
Telford
Shrewsbury

Loch Lomond
Firth of Clyde
Clyde
Tweed

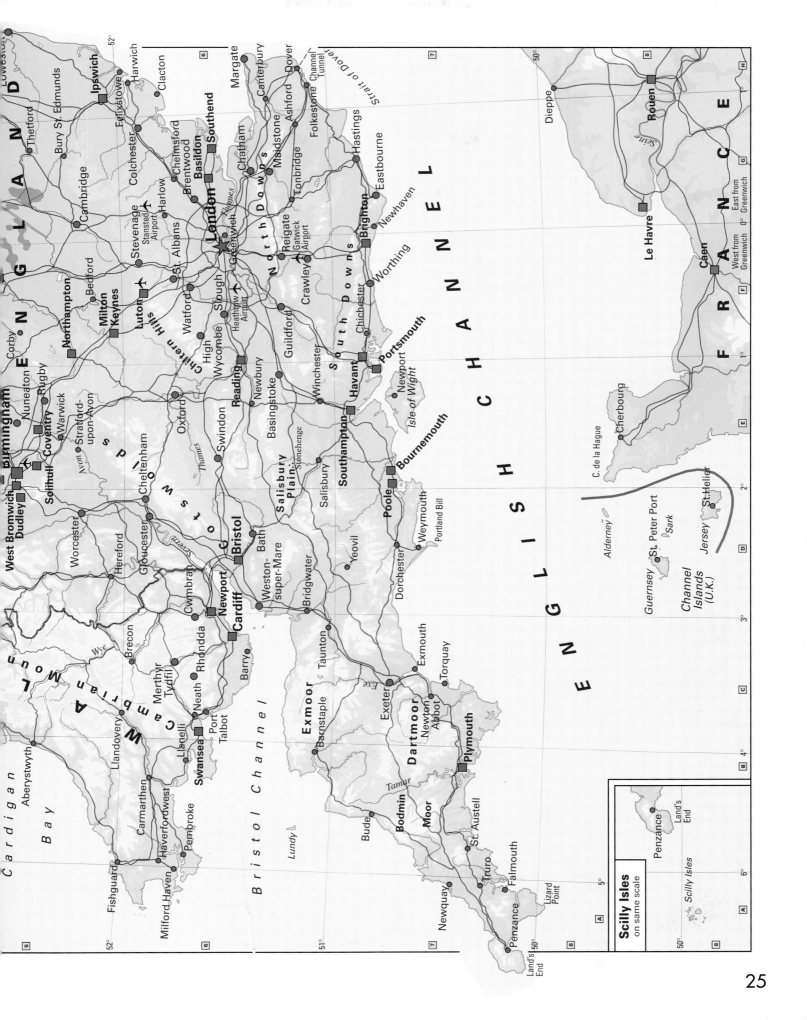

25

Scotland and Ireland

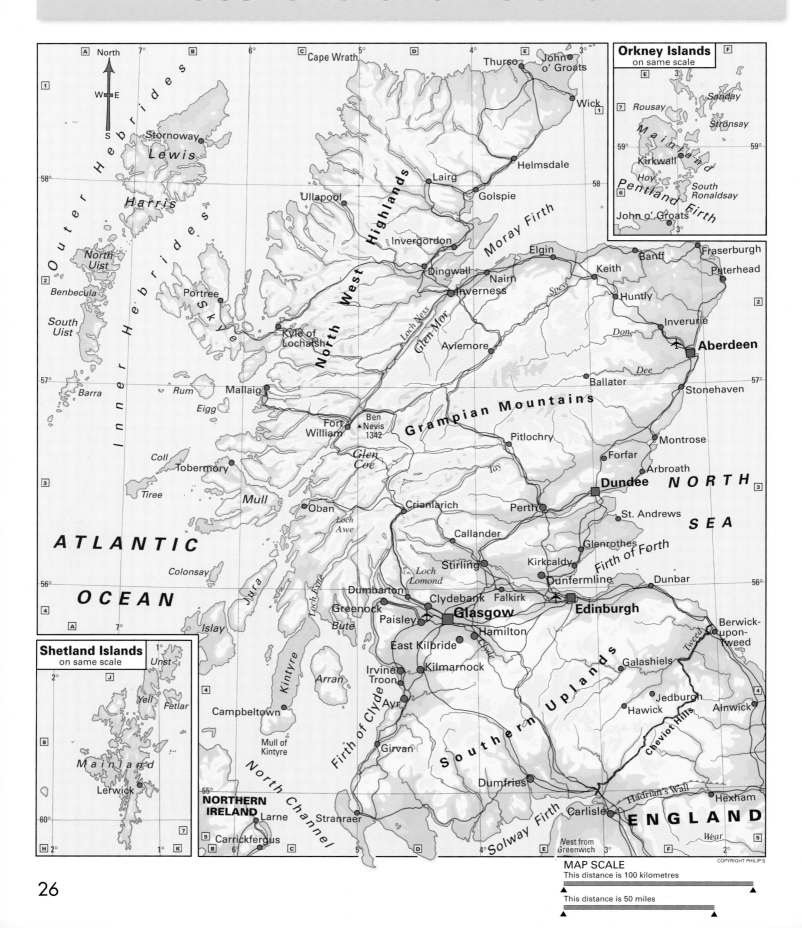

North
W—E
S

Orkney Islands
on same scale

Rousay
Sanday
Stronsay
Mainland
Kirkwall
Hoy
South
Ronaldsay
Pentland Firth
John o' Groats

Cape Wrath
Thurso
John o' Groats
Wick
Helmsdale
Lairg
Golspie
Ullapool
Invergordon
North West Highlands
Moray Firth
Elgin
Banff
Fraserburgh
Peterhead
Dingwall
Nairn
Keith
Huntly
Inverness
Spey
Inverurie
Loch Ness
Glen Mor
Don
Aberdeen
Stornoway
Lewis
Harris
Outer Hebrides
Inner Hebrides
North Uist
Benbecula
South Uist
Barra
Portree
Skye
Kyle of Lochalsh
Aviemore
Dee
Ballater
Stonehaven
Rum
Eigg
Mallaig
Ben Nevis 1342
Grampian Mountains
Montrose
Coll
Tobermory
Fort William
Glen Coe
Pitlochry
Forfar
Arbroath
Tiree
Mull
Oban
Loch Awe
Crianlarich
Tay
Perth
Dundee
St. Andrews
NORTH SEA
Colonsay
ATLANTIC OCEAN
Callander
Glenrothes
Firth of Forth
Stirling
Kirkcaldy
Dunfermline
Dunbar
Loch Lomond
Jura
Loch Fyne
Dumbarton
Clydebank
Falkirk
Edinburgh
Greenock
Glasgow
Paisley
Hamilton
Berwick-upon-Tweed
Bute
East Kilbride
Clyde
Tweed
Islay
Kilmarnock
Galashiels
Arran
Irvine
Troon
Jedburgh
Kintyre
Ayr
Hawick
Alnwick
Campbeltown
Southern Uplands
Cheviot Hills
Mull of Kintyre
Girvan
Firth of Clyde
Dumfries
Hexham
NORTHERN IRELAND
Larne
North Channel
Stranraer
Solway Firth
Carlisle
Hadrian's Wall
ENGLAND
Wear
Carrickfergus
West from Greenwich

Shetland Islands
on same scale

Unst
Yell
Fetlar
Mainland
Lerwick

MAP SCALE
This distance is 100 kilometres
This distance is 50 miles

COPYRIGHT PHILIP'S

26

Map information

Height of land

metres
Over 1000
400–1000
200–400
100–200
0–100
Below sea level
Sea

Rivers
Main roads
Main railways
✈ Main airports
■ ■ ● Cities and towns
★ Capital city
Country boundaries
Lines of latitude and longitude
A 1 Index squares – see index

▲ 1342 Highest point

North
W—E
S

Arran

Campbeltown

Malin Head

Giants Causeway

Inishowen Peninsula

Mull of Kintyre

Bloody Foreland

Buncrana

Coleraine

North Channel

Aran Island

Letterkenny

Londonderry

Bann

Ballymena

Larne

Stranraer

Strabane

Antrim

Donegal Bay

Donegal

Foyle

Omagh

N O R T H E R N

Lough Neagh

Belfast

Bangor

Ulster

I R E L A N D

Lagan

Lisburn

Ards Peninsula

Bundoran

Erne

Lower Lough Erne

Enniskillen

Portadown

Lurgan

Downpatrick

Shannon

Sligo

Monaghan

Armagh

Newry

▲ 852

Mourne Mountains

Mullet Peninsula

Ballina

Charlestown

Boyle

Cavan

Dundalk

I R I S H

Achill Island

Castlebar

Longford

Drogheda

S E A

Westport

An Uaimh

Lough Mask

Roscommon

Lough Ree

Boyne

Mullingar

Lough Corrib

Tuam

Suck

Athlone

L e i n s t e r

Dublin

Dun Laoghaire

C o n n a c h t

Ballinasloe

Tullamore

Liffey

Bray

Galway

Shannon

Birr

I R E L A N D

Galway Bay

Wicklow Mountains

Wicklow

Aran Islands

Lough Derg

Port Laoise

Barrow

Ennis

Killaloe

Nenagh

Carlow

Arklow

Kilrush

Limerick

Thurles

Nore

Shannon

Kilkenny

A T L A N T I C

O C E A N

Tipperary

Suir

Caher

Carrick-on-Suir

Wexford

Rosslare

M u n s t e r

Clonmel

Tralee

Dingle

Knockmealdown Mountains

Waterford

Carnsore Point

Dingle Bay

Mallow

Blackwater

Dungarvan

Killarney

Macgillycuddy's Reeks ▲ 1041

Carrauntoohill

Boggeragh Mountains

Cork

Youghal

Valencia Island

Cobh

Caha Mountains

Bandon

Kenmare

Bantry

Bantry Bay

Cape Clear

C E L T I C   S E A

St. George's Channel

West from Greenwich

The Earth as a planet

Relative sizes of the planets

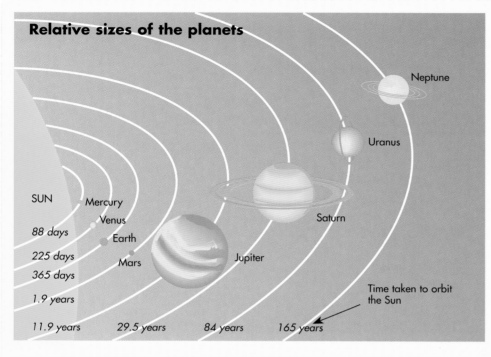

SUN

Mercury

Venus

Earth

Mars

Jupiter

Saturn

Uranus

Neptune

88 days

225 days

365 days

1.9 years

11.9 years   29.5 years   84 years   165 years

Time taken to orbit the Sun

The Solar System

The Earth is one of the eight planets that orbit the Sun. These two diagrams show how big the planets are, how far they are away from the Sun and how long they take to orbit the Sun. The diagram on the left shows how the planets closest to the Sun have the shortest orbits. The Earth takes 365 days (a year) to go round the Sun. The Earth is the fifth largest planet. It is much smaller than Jupiter and Saturn which are the largest planets.

Distances of the planets from the Sun in millions of kilometres

Mercury 58

Venus 108

Earth 150

Mars 228

Asteroids

Jupiter 778

Saturn 1,430

Uranus 2,870

Neptune 4,500

Planet Earth

The Earth spins as if it is on a rod – its axis. The axis would come out of the Earth at two points. The northern point is called the North Pole and the southern point is called the South Pole. The distance between the Poles through the centre of the Earth is 12,700 km.

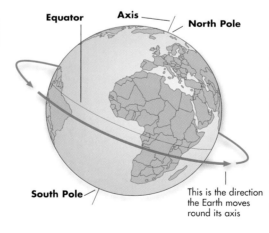

Equator   Axis   North Pole

South Pole

This is the direction the Earth moves round its axis

It takes a day (24 hours) for the Earth to rotate on its axis. It is light (day) when it faces the Sun and dark (night) when it faces away. See the diagram below. The Equator is a line round the Earth which is halfway between the Poles. It is 40,000 km long.

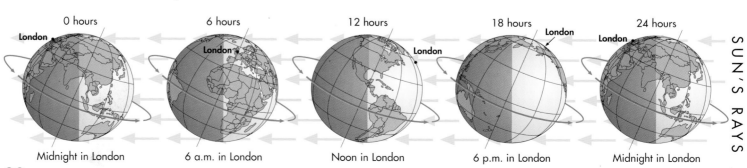

0 hours   6 hours   12 hours   18 hours   24 hours

London   London   London   London   London

Midnight in London   6 a.m. in London   Noon in London   6 p.m. in London   Midnight in London

SUN'S RAYS

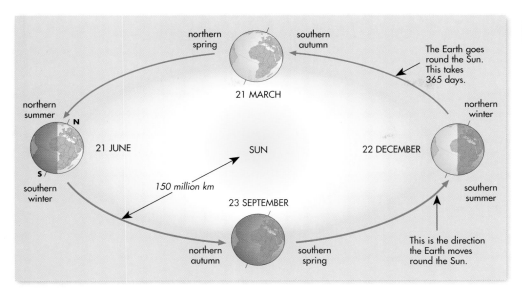

The year and seasons

The Earth is always tilted at $66\frac{1}{2}°$. It moves around the Sun. This movement gives us the seasons of the year. In June the northern hemisphere tilts towards the Sun so it is summer. Six months later, in December, the Earth has rotated halfway round the Sun. It is then summer in the southern hemisphere.

Sun's rays

| | **21 March**
Sun at right angles to tilt | **21 June**
In north, tilt towards the Sun | **23 September**
Sun at right angles to tilt | **22 December**
In north, tilt away from the Sun |
| | In south, tilt away from the Sun | | In south, tilt towards the Sun |

Season	Northern Spring Southern Autumn			Northern Summer Southern Winter			Northern Autumn Southern Spring			Northern Winter Southern Summer		
City	London	Nairobi	Cape Town	London	Nairobi	Cape Town	London	Nairobi	Cape Town	London	Nairobi	Cape Town
Latitude	51°N	1°S	34°S	51°N	1°S	34°S	51°N	1°S	34°S	51°N	1°S	34°S
Day length	12 hrs	12 hrs	12 hrs	16 hrs	12 hrs	10 hrs	12 hrs	12 hrs	12 hrs	8 hrs	12 hrs	14 hrs
Night length	12 hrs	12 hrs	12 hrs	8 hrs	12 hrs	14 hrs	12 hrs	12 hrs	12 hrs	16 hrs	12 hrs	10 hrs
Temperature	7°C	21°C	21°C	16°C	18°C	13°C	15°C	19°C	14°C	5°C	19°C	20°C

For example, at London in spring and autumn there are 12 hours of day and 12 hours of night. In winter this becomes 8 hours and in the summer 16 hours.

The Moon

The Moon is about a quarter the size of the Earth. It orbits the Earth in just over 27 days (almost a month). The Moon is round but we on Earth see only the parts lit by the Sun. This makes it look as if the Moon is a different shape at different times of the month. These are known as the phases of the Moon and they are shown in this diagram.

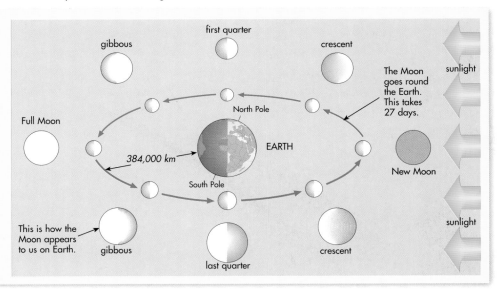

Mountains and rivers

The surface of the Earth is continually being shaped by movements of the Earth's crust. Volcanoes are formed and earthquakes are caused in this way. Rivers also shape the landscape as they flow on their way to the sea.

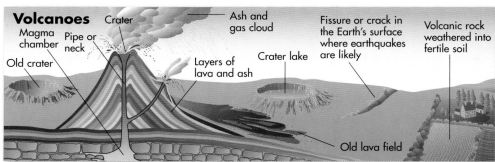

Volcanoes
Crater
Magma chamber
Pipe or neck
Old crater
Ash and gas cloud
Layers of lava and ash
Crater lake
Fissure or crack in the Earth's surface where earthquakes are likely
Volcanic rock weathered into fertile soil
Old lava field

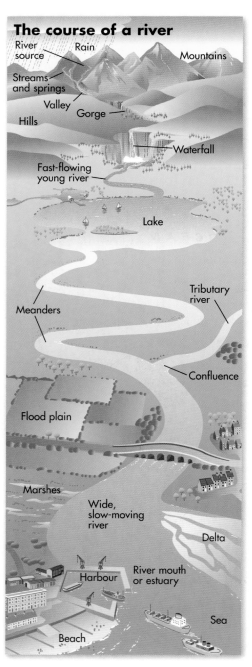

The course of a river
River source
Rain
Mountains
Streams and springs
Valley
Gorge
Hills
Waterfall
Fast-flowing young river
Lake
Meanders
Tributary river
Confluence
Flood plain
Marshes
Wide, slow-moving river
Delta
Harbour
River mouth or estuary
Beach
Sea

Longest rivers

(kilometres)

Nile	6,695
Amazon	6,450
Yangtze	6,380

Highest mountains

(metres)

Everest	8,850
K2	8,611
Kanchenjunga	8,598

Largest lakes

(square metres)

Caspian Sea	371,000
Lake Superior	82,350
Lake Victoria	68,000

Largest islands

(square kilometres)

Greenland	2,175,600
New Guinea	821,030
Borneo	744,360

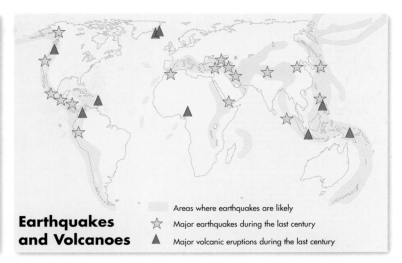

Earthquakes and Volcanoes

- Areas where earthquakes are likely
- ☆ Major earthquakes during the last century
- ▲ Major volcanic eruptions during the last century

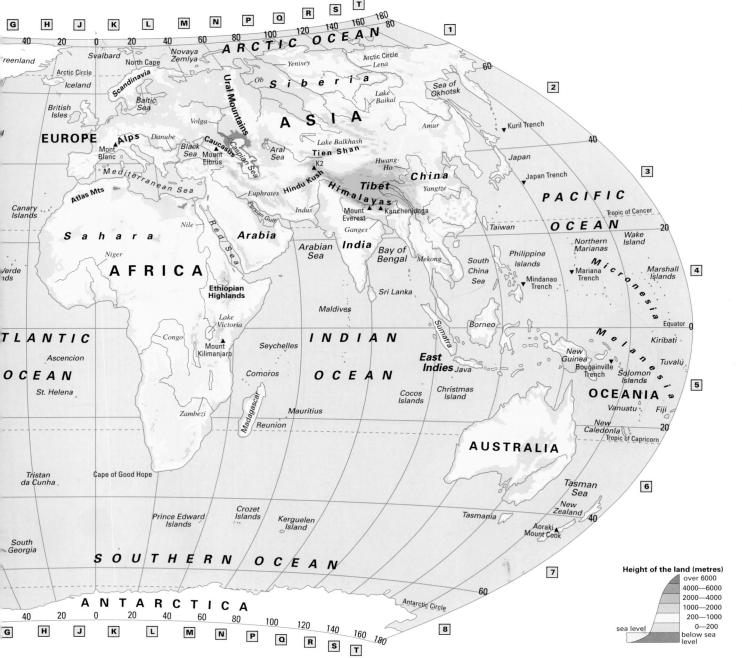

Height of the land (metres)

- over 6000
- 4000—6000
- 2000—4000
- 1000—2000
- 200—1000
- 0—200
- sea level
- below sea level

Climates of the World

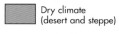

	Tropical climate (hot and wet)		Dry climate (desert and steppe)		Mild climate (warm and wet)		Continental climate (cold and wet)		Polar climate (very cold and dry)		Mountainous areas (where altitude affects climate type)

Heavy rainfall and high temperatures all the year with little difference between the hot and cold months.

Many months, often years, without rain. High temperatures in the summer but cooler in winter.

Rain every month. Warm summers and cool winters.

Mild summers and very cold winters.

Very cold at all times, especially in the winter months. Very little rainfall.

Lower temperatures because the land is high. Heavy rain and snow.

Key to the climate graphs

Total annual rainfall

Average monthly rainfall

Months of the year from January to December

Average monthly temperature in degrees C. When the temperature is below freezing the lines extend below the bottom of the graph.

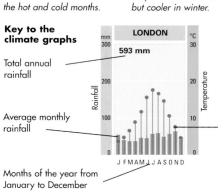

LONDON — 593 mm

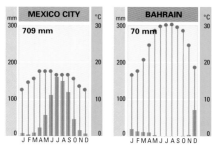

MEXICO CITY — 709 mm
BAHRAIN — 70 mm
MOSCOW — 575 mm   −10°C
CHURCHILL — 410 mm   −28°C

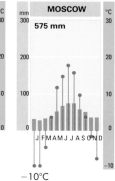

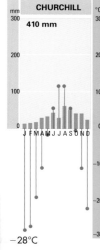

EISMITTE — 5 mm   −45°C

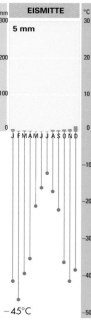

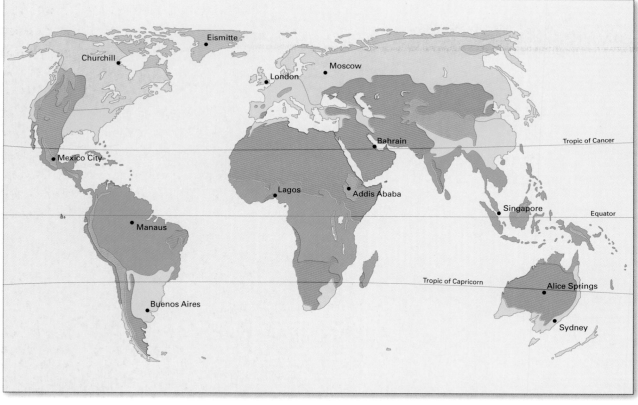

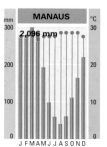

MANAUS — 2,096 mm

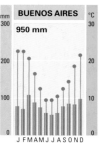

BUENOS AIRES — 950 mm

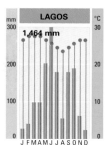

LAGOS — 1,464 mm

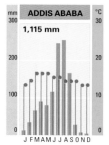

ADDIS ABABA — 1,115 mm

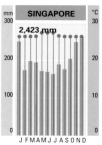

SINGAPORE — 2,423 mm

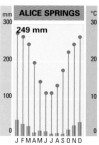

ALICE SPRINGS — 249 mm

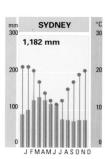

SYDNEY — 1,182 mm

Annual rainfall

Human, plant and animal life cannot live without water. The map on the right shows how much rain falls in different parts of the world. You can see that there is a lot of rain in some places near the Equator. In other places, like the desert areas of the world, there is very little rain. Few plants or animals can survive there. There is also very little rain in the cold lands of the north.

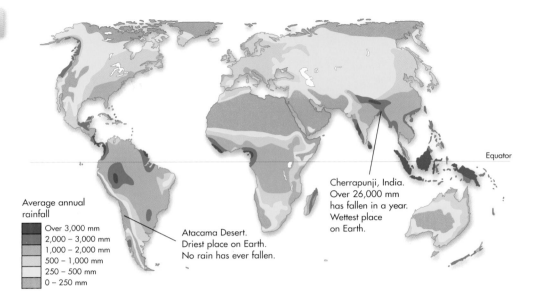

Equator

Average annual rainfall

- Over 3,000 mm
- 2,000 – 3,000 mm
- 1,000 – 2,000 mm
- 500 – 1,000 mm
- 250 – 500 mm
- 0 – 250 mm

Atacama Desert. Driest place on Earth. No rain has ever fallen.

Cherrapunji, India. Over 26,000 mm has fallen in a year. Wettest place on Earth.

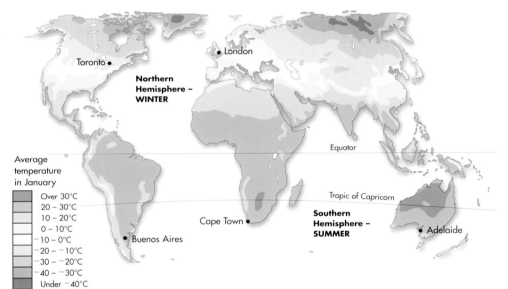

London

Toronto

Northern Hemisphere – WINTER

Equator

Average temperature in January

- Over 30°C
- 20 – 30°C
- 10 – 20°C
- 0 – 10°C
- −10 – 0°C
- −20 – −10°C
- −30 – −20°C
- −40 – −30°C
- Under −40°C

Cape Town

Buenos Aires

Tropic of Capricorn

Southern Hemisphere – SUMMER

Adelaide

January temperature

In December, it is winter in the northern hemisphere. It is hot in the southern continents and cold in the northern continents. The North Pole is tilted away from the sun. It is overhead in the regions around the Tropic of Capricorn. This means that there are about 14 hours of daylight in Buenos Aires, Cape Town and Adelaide, and only about 8 hours in London and Toronto.

June temperature

In June, it is summer in the northern hemisphere and winter in the southern hemisphere. It is warmer in the northern lands and colder in the south. The North Pole is tilted towards the sun. This means that in London and Toronto there are about 16 hours of daylight, but in Buenos Aires, Cape Town and Adelaide there are just under 10 hours.

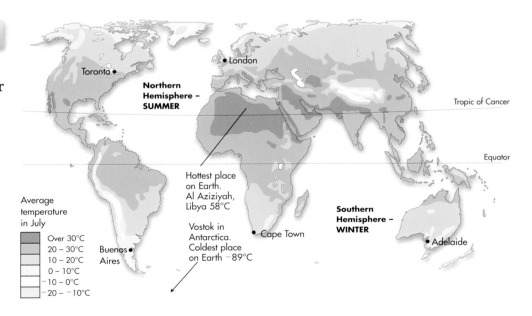

Toronto

London

Northern Hemisphere – SUMMER

Tropic of Cancer

Equator

Hottest place on Earth. Al Aziziyah, Libya 58°C

Vostok in Antarctica. Coldest place on Earth −89°C

Cape Town

Southern Hemisphere – WINTER

Adelaide

Average temperature in July

- Over 30°C
- 20 – 30°C
- 10 – 20°C
- 0 – 10°C
- −10 – 0°C
- −20 – −10°C

Buenos Aires

33

Forests, grasslands and wastes

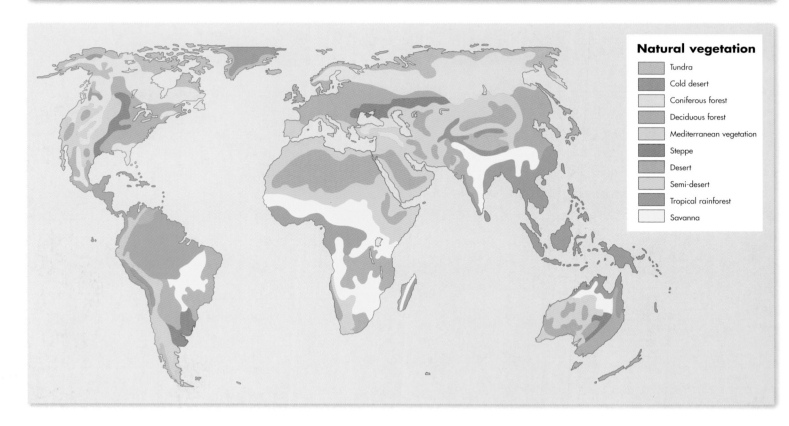

Natural vegetation

- Tundra
- Cold desert
- Coniferous forest
- Deciduous forest
- Mediterranean vegetation
- Steppe
- Desert
- Semi-desert
- Tropical rainforest
- Savanna

The map above shows types of vegetation around the world. The diagram below shows the types of plants which grow on mountains.

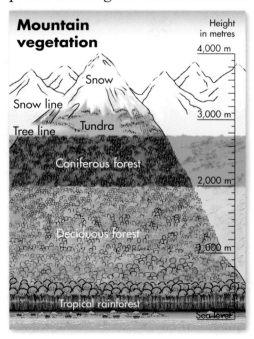

Mountain vegetation

Height in metres

4,000 m

Snow

Snow line

Tree line

Tundra

3,000 m

Coniferous forest

2,000 m

Deciduous forest

1,000 m

Tropical rainforest

Sea level

Tundra

Long, dry, cold winters. Grasses, moss, bog and dwarf trees.

Coniferous forest

Harsh winters, mild summers. Trees have leaves all year.

Mediterranean

Hot, dry summers. Mild wet winters. Plants adapt to the heat.

Desert

Rain is rare. Plants only grow at oases with underground water.

Tropical rainforest (jungle)

Very hot and wet all the year. Tall trees and lush vegetation.

Cold desert

Very cold with little rain or snow. No plants can grow.

Deciduous forest

Rain all year, cool winters. Trees shed leaves in winter.

Steppe

Some rain with a dry season. Grasslands with some trees.

Semi-desert

Poor rains, sparse vegetation. Grass with a few small trees.

Savanna

Mainly dry, but lush grass grows when the rains come.

Tundra

Pingo (mound)

Thin, stony soil with permafrost below

Mosses, lichens and herbs

Cold desert

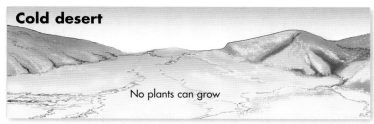

No plants can grow

Coniferous forest

Evergreen conifers (spruces and firs)

Young tree saplings and small shrubs

Carpet of pine needles

Ferns and brambles on edge of forest

Yearly cycle of a deciduous forest

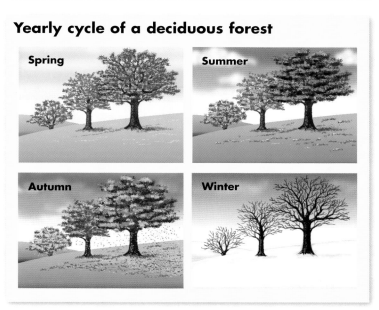

Spring

Summer

Autumn

Winter

Mediterranean

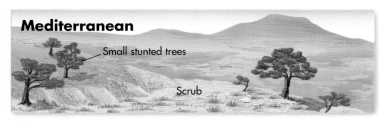

Small stunted trees

Scrub

Steppe

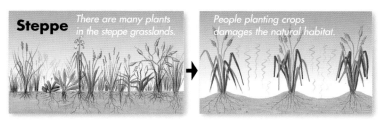

There are many plants in the steppe grasslands.

People planting crops damages the natural habitat.

Tropical rainforest

Scattered trees with umbrella-shaped tops grow the highest.

Main layer of tall trees growing close together.

Creepers grow up the trees to reach the sunlight.

Ferns, mosses and small plants grow closest to the ground.

Desert

Cactus

Sand blown into dunes by the wind

Palm trees

Oasis

Semi-desert

Grass and bush

Joshua trees

Savanna

Dry season

Wet season

Agriculture, forests and fishing

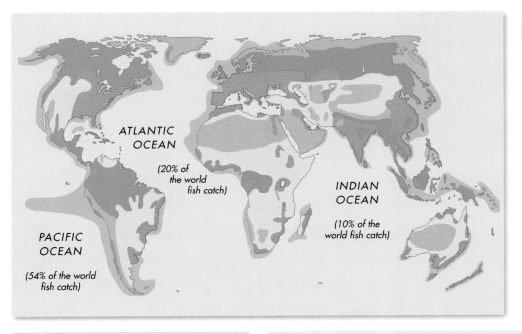

ATLANTIC OCEAN

(20% of the world fish catch)

INDIAN OCEAN

(10% of the world fish catch)

PACIFIC OCEAN

(54% of the world fish catch)

How the land is used

Forest areas with timber. Some hunting and fishing. Agriculture in the tropics.

Deserts and wastelands. Some small areas of agriculture in oases or places that have been irrigated.

Animal farming on large farms (ranches)

Farming of crops and animals on large and small farms

Main fishing areas

The importance of agriculture

Over half the people work in agriculture

Between a quarter and half the people work in agriculture

Between one in ten and a quarter of the people work in agriculture

Less than one in ten of the people work in agriculture

● Countries which depend on agriculture for over half their income

A hundred years ago about 80% of the world's population worked in agriculture. Today it is only about 40% but agriculture is still very important in some countries.

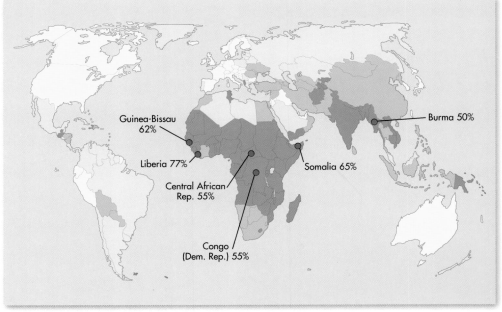

Guinea-Bissau 62%

Liberia 77%

Central African Rep. 55%

Somalia 65%

Burma 50%

Congo (Dem. Rep.) 55%

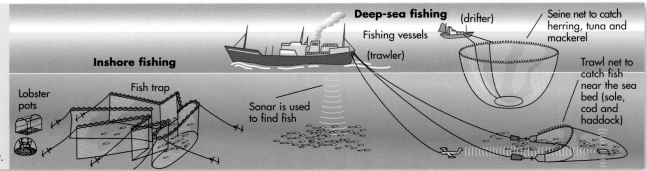

Methods of fishing

There are two types of sea fishing:

1. **Deep-sea fishing** using large trawlers which often stay at sea for many weeks.

2. **Inshore fishing** using small boats, traps and nets up to 70 km from the coast.

Inshore fishing

Lobster pots

Fish trap

Sonar is used to find fish

Deep-sea fishing

Fishing vessels

(drifter)

(trawler)

Seine net to catch herring, tuna and mackerel

Trawl net to catch fish near the sea bed (sole, cod and haddock)

Wheat and rice

- One dot stands for 4 million tonnes of wheat produced
- One dot stands for 4 million tonnes of rice produced

Wheat is the main cereal crop grown in cooler regions. Rice is the main food for over half the people in the world. It is grown in water in paddy fields in tropical areas. Nearly a third of the world's rice is grown in China.

Cattle and sheep

- One dot stands for 10 million cattle
- One dot stands for 10 million sheep

Meat, milk and leather come from cattle. The map shows that they are kept in most parts of the world except where it is hot or very cold. Sheep are kept in cooler regions and they can live on poorer grassland than cows. Sheep are reared for meat and wool.

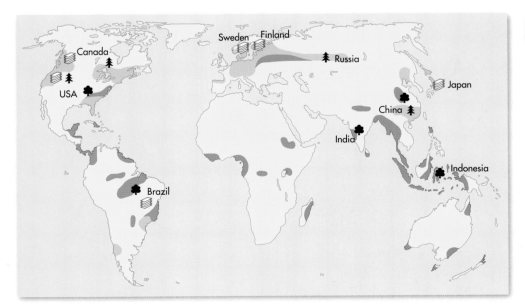

Timber

- Main areas where trees are grown for hardwoods (non-coniferous)
- Main areas where trees are grown for softwoods (coniferous)

Countries producing over 5% of
- ♣ the world's hardwood
- ♠ the world's softwood
- ▧ the world's wood pulp

Trees are cut down to make timber. Softwood trees such as pines and firs often have cones so they are called coniferous. Some trees are chopped up into wood pulp which is used to make paper.

Minerals and energy

Important metals

- ■ Iron ore
- ▲ Bauxite
- ● Copper

Iron is the most important metal in manufacturing. It is mixed with other metals to make steel which is used for ships, cars and machinery. Bauxite ore is used to make aluminium. Aluminium is light and strong. It is used to make aeroplanes. Copper is used for electric wires, and also to make brass and bronze.

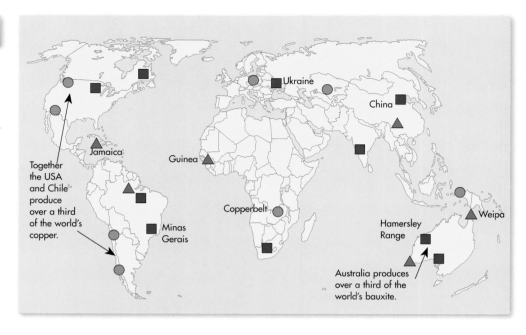

Together the USA and Chile produce over a third of the world's copper.

Australia produces over a third of the world's bauxite.

Ukraine · China · Jamaica · Guinea · Copperbelt · Hamersley Range · Weipa · Minas Gerais

Precious metals and minerals

- ▱ Gold
- ★ Silver
- ◆ Diamonds

Some minerals like gold, silver and diamonds are used to make jewellery. They are also important in industry. Diamonds are the hardest mineral and so they are used on tools that cut or grind. Silver is used in photography to coat film, and to make electrical goods. Gold is used in the electronics industry.

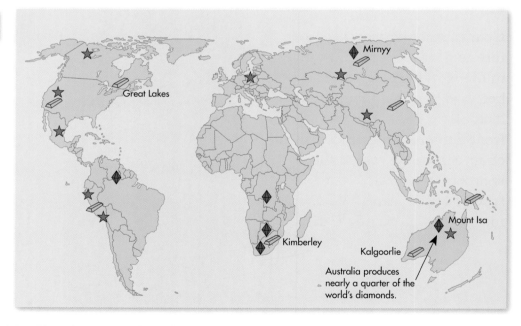

Great Lakes · Mirnyy · Kimberley · Kalgoorlie · Mount Isa

Australia produces nearly a quarter of the world's diamonds.

There are over 70 different types of metals and minerals in the world. The maps above show the main countries where some of the most important ones are mined. After mining, metals and fuels are often exported to other countries where they are manufactured into goods. The map on the left shows which countries depend most on mining for their exports and wealth. These countries are coloured red.

Oil and gas

🛢 Oilfields

🌀 Natural gasfields

➡ Main routes for transporting oil and gas by tanker

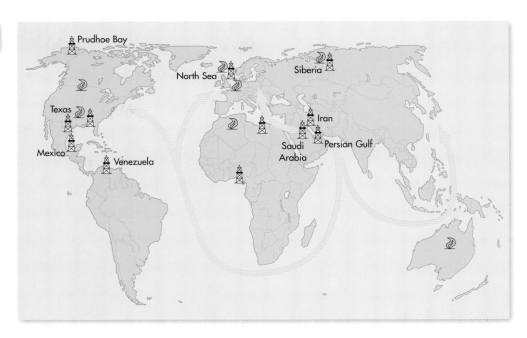

Crude oil is drilled from deep in the Earth's crust. The oil is then refined so that it can be used in different industries. Oil is used to make petrol and is also very important in the chemical industry. Natural gas is often found in the same places as oil.

Coal

▲ Lignite (soft brown coal)

▲ Hard coal (bituminous)

➡ Main routes for transporting coal

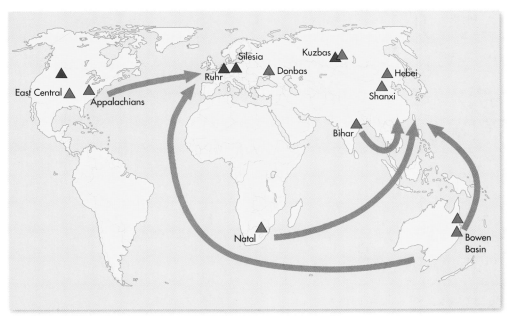

Coal is a fuel that comes from forests and swamps that rotted millions of years ago and have been crushed by layers of rock. The coal is cut out of the rock from deep mines and also from open-cast mines where the coal is nearer the surface. The oldest type of coal is hard. The coal formed more recently is softer.

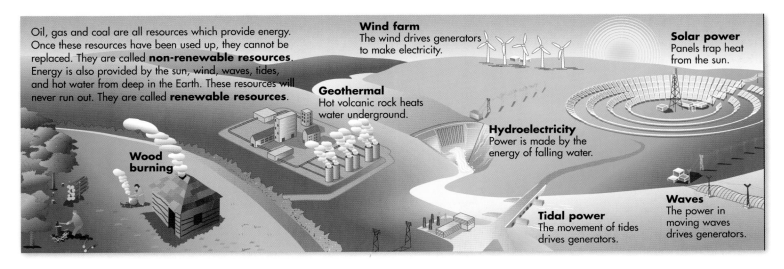

Oil, gas and coal are all resources which provide energy. Once these resources have been used up, they cannot be replaced. They are called **non-renewable resources**. Energy is also provided by the sun, wind, waves, tides, and hot water from deep in the Earth. These resources will never run out. They are called **renewable resources**.

Wood burning

Geothermal
Hot volcanic rock heats water underground.

Wind farm
The wind drives generators to make electricity.

Hydroelectricity
Power is made by the energy of falling water.

Tidal power
The movement of tides drives generators.

Waves
The power in moving waves drives generators.

Solar power
Panels trap heat from the sun.

39

Peoples and cities of the World

Where people live

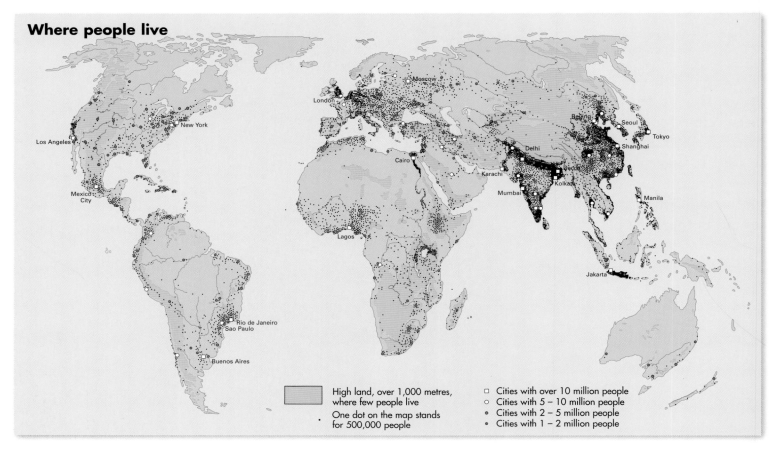

High land, over 1,000 metres, where few people live

. One dot on the map stands for 500,000 people

□ Cities with over 10 million people
○ Cities with 5 – 10 million people
• Cities with 2 – 5 million people
• Cities with 1 – 2 million people

The growth of the population of the world 1000 – 2008 AD

The population of the continents (2006)

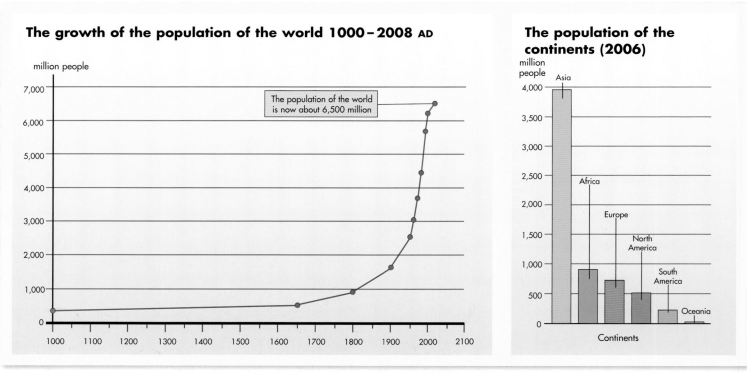

The population of the world is now about 6,500 million

Population by continents

In this diagram the size of each continent is in proportion to its population.

Each square represents 1% of the world population of 6,500 million.

Population of countries in millions

China	1,314
India	1,095
USA	301
Indonesia	245
Brazil	188
Pakistan	166
Bangladesh	147
Russia	143
Nigeria	132
Japan	127
Mexico	107
Philippines	89
Vietnam	84
Germany	82
Egypt	79
Ethiopia	75
Turkey	70
Iran	69
Thailand	65

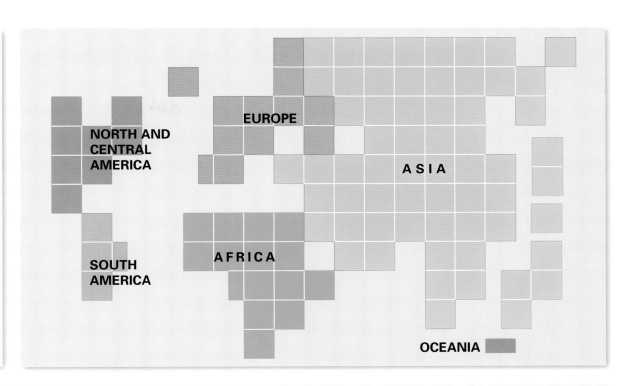

NORTH AND CENTRAL AMERICA

EUROPE

ASIA

SOUTH AMERICA

AFRICA

OCEANIA

Cities of the World

More people live in cities and towns than in the countryside. These maps show four of the world's largest cities.

- Built-up area – houses, shops and factories
- Poor housing – slums
- City centre – big shops, offices and government buildings
- Parks and woodland
- Favelas – areas of poor housing in Rio de Janeiro
- ✈ International airport
- — Major roads

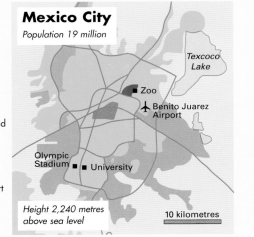

Mexico City
Population 19 million

Texcoco Lake

Zoo
✈ Benito Juarez Airport

Olympic Stadium ■ University

Height 2,240 metres above sea level

10 kilometres

Shanghai
Population 13 million

Yangtze River

Wusong

Nanxi'ang

■ Tomb of Lu Xun

Wusong River

People's Park

Yuyuan Garden

✈ Zoo

Pudong New Area

Huangpu River

10 kilometres

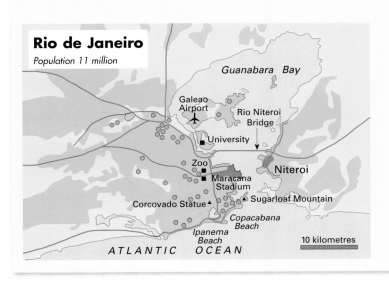

Rio de Janeiro
Population 11 million

Guanabara Bay

Galeao Airport

Rio Niteroi Bridge

■ University

Zoo

Niteroi

Maracana Stadium

Corcovado Statue ▲

▲ Sugarloaf Mountain

Copacabana Beach

Ipanema Beach

ATLANTIC OCEAN

10 kilometres

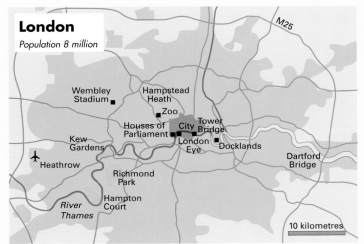

London
Population 8 million

M25

Wembley Stadium ■

Hampstead Heath

Zoo

Houses of Parliament

City

Tower Bridge

Kew Gardens

London Eye

Docklands

✈ Heathrow

Richmond Park

Dartford Bridge

Hampton Court

River Thames

10 kilometres

Transport and communication

Seaways

— Main shipping routes

■ The biggest seaports in the world (over a hundred million tonnes of cargo handled a year)

● Other big seaports

▱ Ice and icebergs in the sea all the time, or for some part of the year

— Large ships can sail on these rivers

Sea transport is used for goods that are too bulky or heavy to go by air. The main shipping routes are between North America, Europe and the Far East.

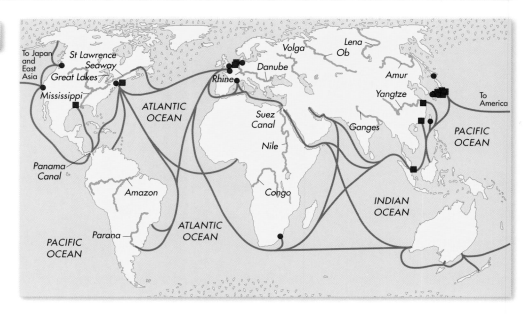

The Panama Canal

Opened in 1914
82 km long
14,000 ships a year

The Suez Canal

Opened in 1870
162 km long
18,000 ships a year

These two important canals cut through narrow pieces of land. Can you work out how much shorter the journeys are by using the canals?

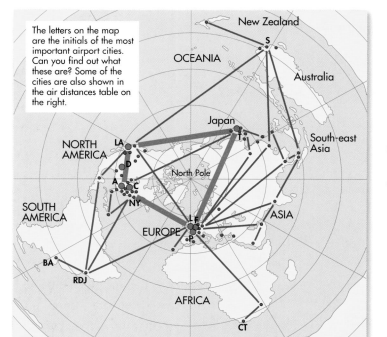

The letters on the map are the initials of the most important airport cities. Can you find out what these are? Some of the cities are also shown in the air distances table on the right.

● Large international airports (over 50 million passengers a year)

· Other important airports

━ Heavily used air routes

— Other important air routes

Airways

This map has the North Pole at its centre. It shows how much air traffic connects Europe, North America, Japan and Eastern Asia. You can see the long distances in the USA and Russia that are covered by air.

Air distances (kilometres)

	Buenos Aires	Cape Town	London	Los Angeles	New York	Sydney	Tokyo
Buenos Aires		6,880	11,128	9,854	8,526	11,760	18,338
Cape Town	6,880		9,672	16,067	12,551	10,982	14,710
London	11,128	9,672		8,752	5,535	17,005	9,584
Los Angeles	9,854	16,067	8,752		3,968	12,052	8,806
New York	8,526	12,551	5,535	3,968		16,001	10,869
Sydney	11,760	10,982	17,005	12,052	16,001		7,809
Tokyo	18,338	14,710	9,584	8,806	10,869	7,809	

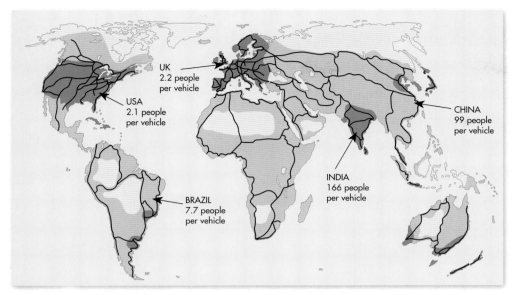

Roads

▨	Many roads and motorways
▨	Not many roads, few with hard surfaces and many only tracks. Many roads are through-routes.
☐	No roads or very few roads
—	Important long-distance roads

This map shows some of the major roads that link important cities and ports. It also shows how many people there are in proportion to the number of vehicles in some countries.

UK
2.2 people
per vehicle

USA
2.1 people
per vehicle

CHINA
99 people
per vehicle

INDIA
166 people
per vehicle

BRAZIL
7.7 people
per vehicle

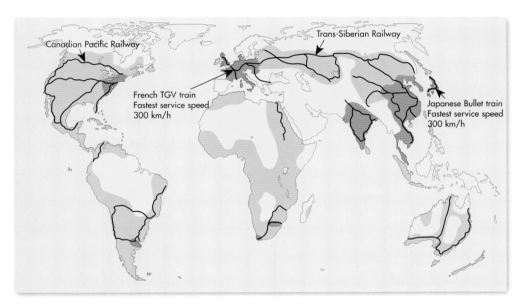

Railways

▨	Many passenger and goods lines
▨	Scattered railways often taking goods to and from parts of the coast
☐	No rail services or very few rail services
—	Important long-distance railways

This map shows some of the important long-distance railways in the world. Railways are often used for transporting goods between cities and to ports.

Canadian Pacific Railway

Trans-Siberian Railway

French TGV train
Fastest service speed
300 km/h

Japanese Bullet train
Fastest service speed
300 km/h

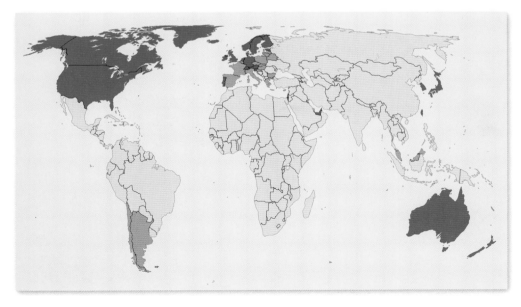

Internet

▨	Over half the population use the internet
▨	Between a quarter and a half of the population use the internet
☐	Under a quarter of the population use the internet

The internet started in the 1960s and has now grown into a huge network with over 1.3 billion users around the world. The most popular uses of the internet are email and the world wide web.

Global warming

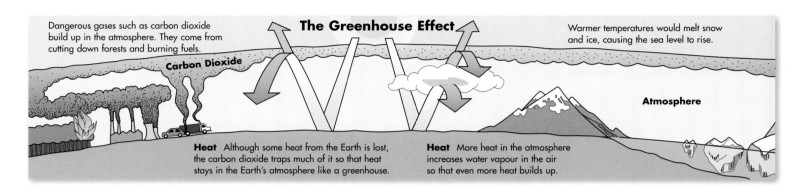

The Greenhouse Effect

Dangerous gases such as carbon dioxide build up in the atmosphere. They come from cutting down forests and burning fuels.

Carbon Dioxide

Warmer temperatures would melt snow and ice, causing the sea level to rise.

Atmosphere

Heat Although some heat from the Earth is lost, the carbon dioxide traps much of it so that heat stays in the Earth's atmosphere like a greenhouse.

Heat More heat in the atmosphere increases water vapour in the air so that even more heat builds up.

Equator

Carbon dioxide

Major producers of carbon dioxide

Other producers of carbon dioxide

Countries producing very little carbon dioxide

This map shows who produces the most carbon dioxide per person. The countries that contribute the most to global warming tend to be rich countries like the USA and Australia. Can you think of reasons why?

Global warming

Experts have studied climate data all around the world. They agreed several years ago that climate change really was happening. Leaders of all the major countries in the world came together in Kyoto in Japan to try and agree on what to do about it. This graph shows how temperatures might not rise as much if countries can cut their carbon dioxide emissions.

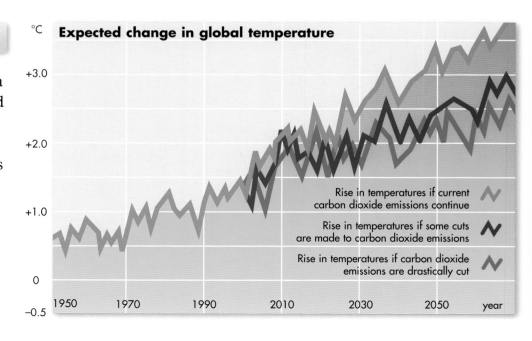

°C **Expected change in global temperature**

+3.0

+2.0

+1.0

0

−0.5

1950   1970   1990   2010   2030   2050   year

Rise in temperatures if current carbon dioxide emissions continue

Rise in temperatures if some cuts are made to carbon dioxide emissions

Rise in temperatures if carbon dioxide emissions are drastically cut

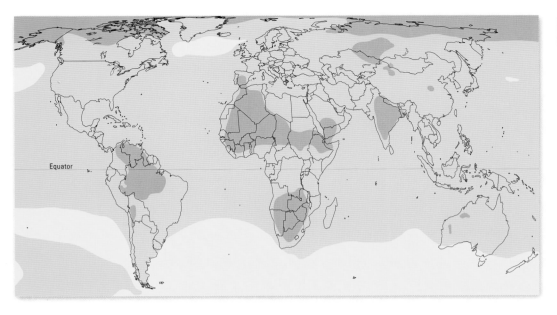

Temperature change

The expected change in temperature in the next 100 years

- More than 5°C warmer
- Betweeen 2°C and 5°C warmer
- Less than 2°C warmer

Compare this map with the map on the opposite page. The countries most affected by temperature change may not be the countries that are causing it.

Rainfall change

The expected change in the amount of rainfall in the next 100 years

- More rainfall
- Very little change in the amount of rainfall
- Less rainfall

As the global climate changes, some parts of the world will get more rainfall, while other parts will become drier. Can you think of the effects this might have?

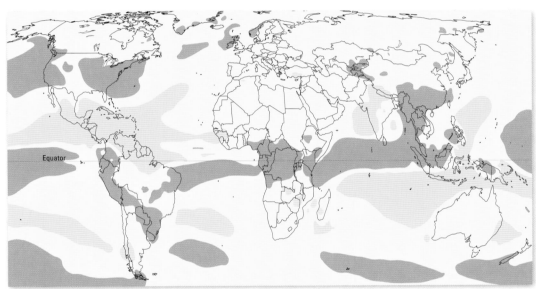

Sea level rise

- Areas at risk from rising sea level
- Areas with many low-lying islands

Warmer temperatures will result in ice caps melting in Antarctica and Greenland. Sea levels will rise and threaten low-lying coastal areas and islands. Some small islands in the Pacific have already disappeared.

Rich and poor

All countries have both rich and poor people but some countries have more poor people than others. The amount of food that people have to eat and the age that they die can often depend on where they live in the world. The world can be divided into two parts – the rich and the poor.

The richer countries are mostly in the North and the poorer countries are mostly in the South. The map below shows which countries are rich and which are poor. The list on the right shows some contrasts between rich and poor. Some of these contrasts can be seen in the maps on these pages.

Rich	Poor
Healthy	Poor health
Educated	Poor education
Well fed	Poorly fed
Small families	Large families
Many industries	Few industries
Few farmers	Many farmers
Give aid	Receive aid

The South has over three-quarters of the world's population but less than a quarter of its wealth.

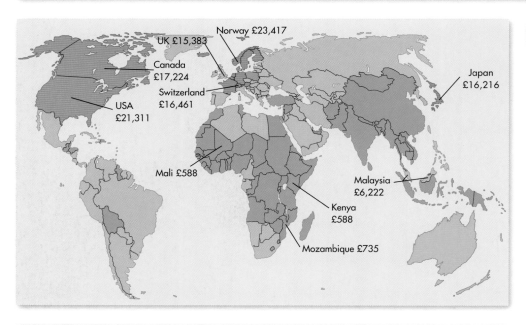

Norway £23,417
UK £15,383
Canada £17,224
Switzerland £16,461
USA £21,311
Japan £16,216
Mali £588
Malaysia £6,222
Kenya £588
Mozambique £735

Income

- Very rich countries
- Rich countries
- Poor countries
- Very poor countries

The map shows how much money there is to spend on each person in a country. This is called income per person – this is worked out by dividing the wealth of a country by its population. The map gives examples of rich and poor countries.

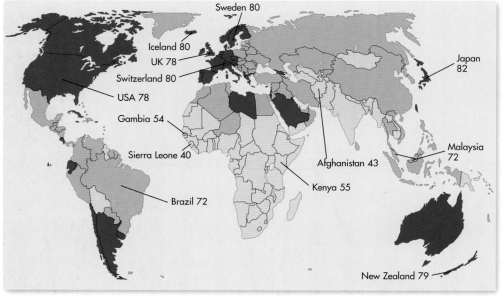

Sweden 80
Iceland 80
UK 78
Switzerland 80
USA 78
Gambia 54
Sierra Leone 40
Brazil 72
Afghanistan 43
Kenya 55
Japan 82
Malaysia 72
New Zealand 79

How long do people live?

This is the average age when people die

- Over 75 years
- 60 – 75 years
- Under 60 years

The average age of death is called life expectancy. In the world as a whole, the average life expectancy is 65 years. Some of the highest and lowest ages of death are shown on the map.

Food and famine

Below the amount of food they need

Above the amount of food they need

Over a third above the amount of food they need

  Major famines since 1980

If people do not have enough to eat they become unhealthy. This map shows where in the world people have less than and more than the amount of food they need to live a healthy life.

Reading and writing

Over half the adults cannot read or write

Between a quarter and a half of the adults cannot read or write

Less than a quarter of the adults cannot read or write

The map shows the proportion of adults in each country who cannot read or write a simple sentence. Can you think of some reasons why more people cannot read or write in some places in the world than in others?

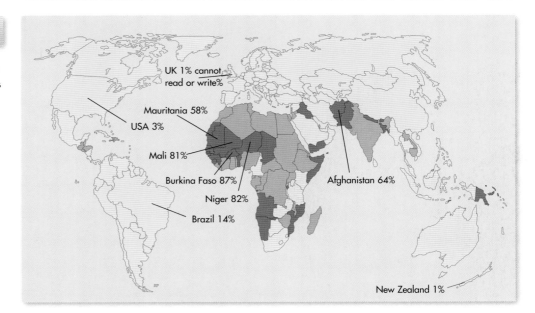

UK 1% cannot read or write%

Mauritania 58%

USA 3%

Mali 81%

Burkina Faso 87%

Niger 82%

Brazil 14%

Afghanistan 64%

New Zealand 1%

Development aid

Over £25 received per person each year

Up to £25 received per person each year

Up to £100 given per person each year

Over £100 given per person each year

Countries that receive or give no aid

Some countries receive aid from other countries. Money is one type of aid. It is used to help with food, health and education problems. The map shows how much different countries give or receive.

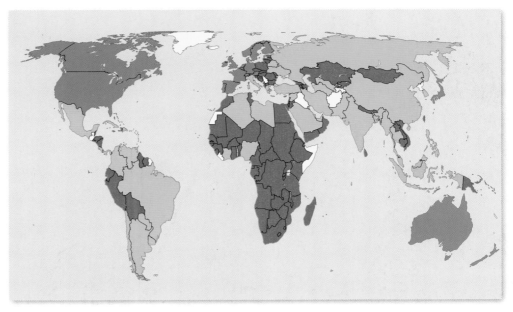

47

Countries of the World

North America

(see pages 58–59)

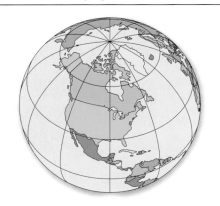

South America

(see pages 60–61)

Africa

(see pages 54–55)

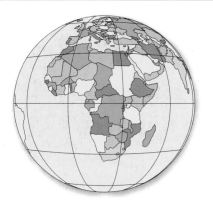

These pages show different maps of the world. The large map shows the world cut through the Pacific Ocean and opened out on to flat paper. The smaller maps of the continents are views of the globe looking down on each of the continents.

Larger maps of the continents appear on the following pages. They show more cities than on this map

Alaska (U.S.A.)

CANADA

UNITED STATES

New York

Los Angeles

Bermuda (U.K.)

ATL

N

Tropic of Cancer

BAHAMAS

CUBA

MEXICO

Hawaiian Islands (U.S.A.)

Mexico City

JAMAICA HAITI DOM. REP.
BELIZE
GUATEMALA HONDURAS
EL SALVADOR   NICARAGUA

Puerto Rico (U.S.A.)

ST. KITTS & NEVIS
ANTIGUA & BARBUDA
DOMINICA
ST. LUCIA
ST. VINCENT   BARBADOS
TRINIDAD & TOBAGO

O

COSTA RICA
PANAMA

VENEZUELA

GUYANA
SURINAME
FRENCH GUIANA

COLOMBIA

P A C I F I C

Kiritimati

Equator

Phoenix Islands

K I R I B A T I

Galapagos Islands (Ecuador)

ECUADOR

BRAZIL

International Date Line

Tokelau Islands (N.Z.)

Marquesas Islands (France)

PERU

SAMOA American Samoa (U.S.A.)

Society Islands (France)

FRENCH POLYNESIA

O C E A N

BOLIVIA

TONGA Cook Islands (N.Z.)

Tahiti (France)

Tuamotu Archipelago (France)

Sao Paulo

Ri
Ja

PARAGUAY

Tubuai Islands (France)

Tropic of Capricorn

Pitcairn Island (U.K.)

Easter Island (Chile)

ARGENTINA

URUGUAY
Buenos Aires

Kermadec Islands (N.Z.)

CHILE

Chatham Islands (N.Z.)

Falkla

Antarctic Circle

■ Cities with more than 10 million people

Europe
(see pages 50–51)

Asia
(see pages 52–53)

Oceania
(see pages 56–57)

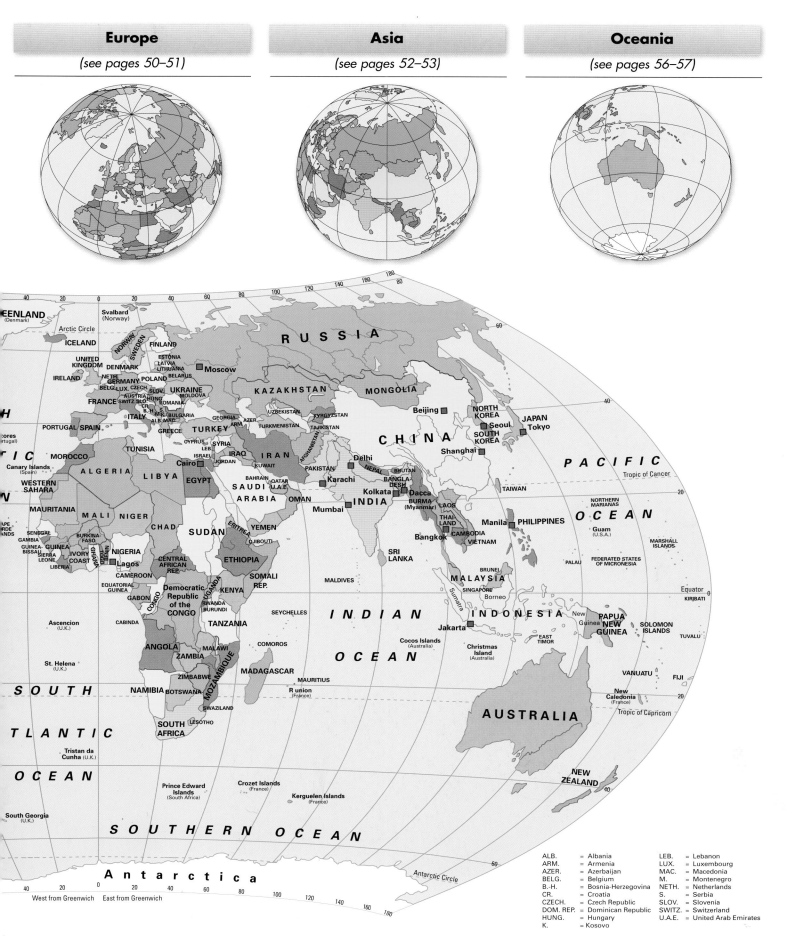

ALB.	= Albania
ARM.	= Armenia
AZER.	= Azerbaijan
BELG.	= Belgium
B.-H.	= Bosnia-Herzegovina
CR.	= Croatia
CZECH.	= Czech Republic
DOM. REP.	= Dominican Republic
HUNG.	= Hungary
K.	= Kosovo

LEB.	= Lebanon
LUX.	= Luxembourg
MAC.	= Macedonia
M.	= Montenegro
NETH.	= Netherlands
S.	= Serbia
SLOV.	= Slovenia
SWITZ.	= Switzerland
U.A.E.	= United Arab Emirates

Europe

Largest countries – by area
(thousand square kilometres)

Russia	17,075
Ukraine	604
France	552
Spain	498

Largest countries – by population
(million people)

Russia	143
Germany	82
France	61
United Kingdom	61

Largest cities
(million people)

Moscow (RUSSIA)	10.7
Paris (FRANCE)	9.6
Istanbul (TURKEY)	9.0
London (UK)	9.0

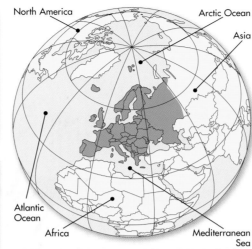

- *Europe is the second smallest continent. It is one fifth the size of Asia. Australia is slightly smaller than Europe.*
- *Great Britain is the largest island in Europe.*
- *Some people think that the whole of Turkey and Cyprus should be included in Europe.*

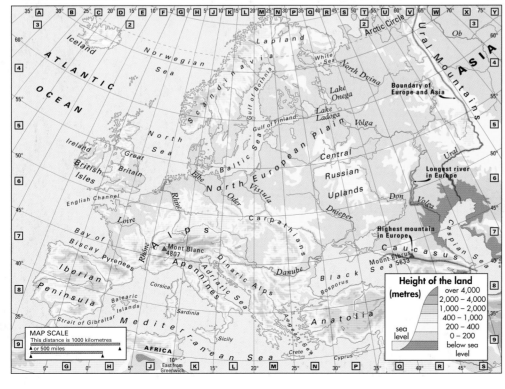

MAP SCALE
This distance is 1000 kilometres or 500 miles

Height of the land (metres)
over 4,000
2,000 – 4,000
1,000 – 2,000
400 – 1,000
200 – 400
sea level 0 – 200
below sea level

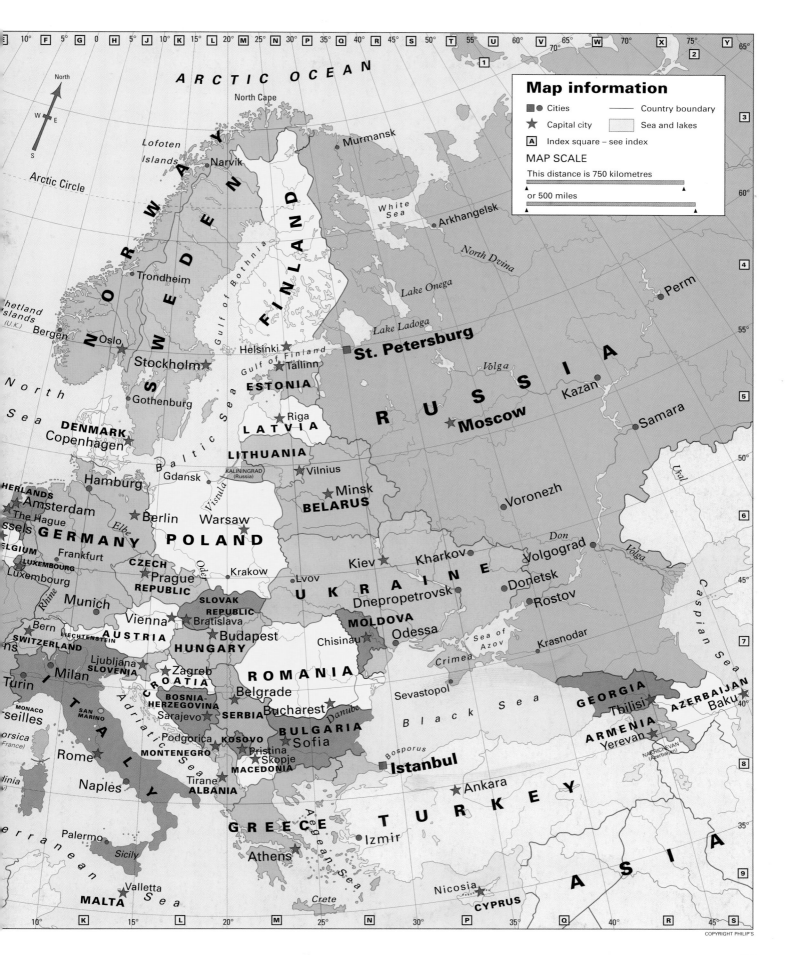

ARCTIC OCEAN

North Cape

Map information

- Cities
- ★ Capital city
- A Index square – see index
- —— Country boundary
- Sea and lakes

MAP SCALE

This distance is 750 kilometres

or 500 miles

North

Lofoten
Islands

Narvik

Murmansk

Arctic Circle

Shetland
Islands
(U.K.)
Bergen

Trondheim

Gulf of Bothnia

White
Sea

Arkhangelsk

North Dvina

Lake Onega

Lake Ladoga

Perm

Oslo

Helsinki

St. Petersburg

Volga

R U S S I A

Stockholm

Tallinn

ESTONIA

Kazan

North
Sea

Gothenburg

Riga

Moscow

Samara

DENMARK
Copenhagen

LATVIA

LITHUANIA

Hamburg

Gdansk

KALININGRAD
(Russia)

Vilnius

Minsk

Voronezh

HERLANDS
Amsterdam
The Hague
ssels
GERMANY

Berlin

Warsaw

BELARUS

Ural

BELGIUM

Elbe

POLAND

Don

Volga

LUXEMBOURG

Frankfurt

CZECH

Oder

Lvov

Kiev

Kharkov

Volgograd

Luxembourg

Rhine

Prague
REPUBLIC

Krakow

U K R A I N E

Donetsk

Caspian Sea

Munich

SLOVAK
REPUBLIC

Dnepropetrovsk

Rostov

Bern
SWITZERLAND
LIECHTENSTEIN

Vienna

Bratislava

AUSTRIA

Budapest

MOLDOVA

Odessa

Krasnodar

ns

Ljubljana
SLOVENIA

HUNGARY

Chisinau

Sea of
Azov

Turin

Milan

Zagreb
CROATIA

ROMANIA

Crimea

MONACO
seilles

SAN
MARINO

Belgrade

Bucharest

Sevastopol

GEORGIA

Tbilisi

AZERBAIJAN
Baku

orsica
(France)

Adriatic

BOSNIA-
HERZEGOVINA
Sarajevo

SERBIA

Danube

Black Sea

ARMENIA
Yerevan

Rome

I T A L Y

Podgorica

KOSOVO
Pristina

BULGARIA
Sofia

Bosporus

NACHICHEVAN
(Azerbaijan)

MONTENEGRO

Istanbul

Naples

Skopje

MACEDONIA

dinia

Sea

Tirane
ALBANIA

GREECE

T U R K E Y

Ankara

A S I A

erranean

Palermo

Sicily

Aegean
Sea

Izmir

MALTA

Valletta
Sea

Athens

Crete

Nicosia

CYPRUS

COPYRIGHT PHILIP'S

51

Asia

Largest countries – by area

(thousand square kilometres)

Russia	17,075
China	9,597
India	3,287

Largest countries – by population

(million people)

China	1,314
India	1,095
Indonesia	245
Russia	143

Largest cities

(million people)

Mumbai (INDIA)	18.3
Delhi (INDIA)	15.3
Kolkata (INDIA)	14.3
Shanghai (CHINA)	12.7
Dacca (BANGLADESH)	12.6

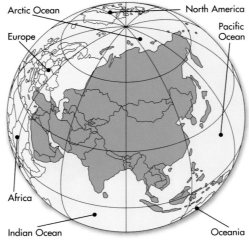

- ■ *Asia is the largest continent. It is twice the size of North America.*
- ■ *It is a continent of long rivers. Many of Asia's rivers are longer than Europe's longest rivers.*
- ■ *Asia contains well over half the world's population.*

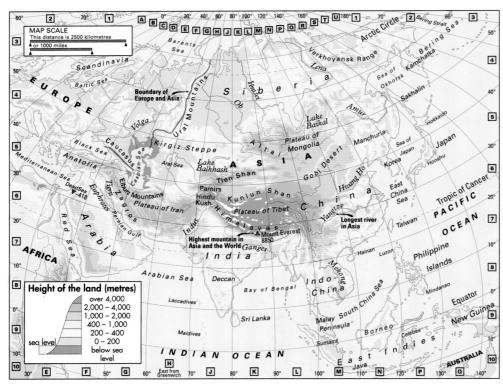

Map information

- ■● Cities
- ★ Capital city
- Ⓐ Index square – see index
- —— Country boundary
- ▭ Sea and lakes

MAP SCALE

This distance is 2000 kilometres

or 1000 miles

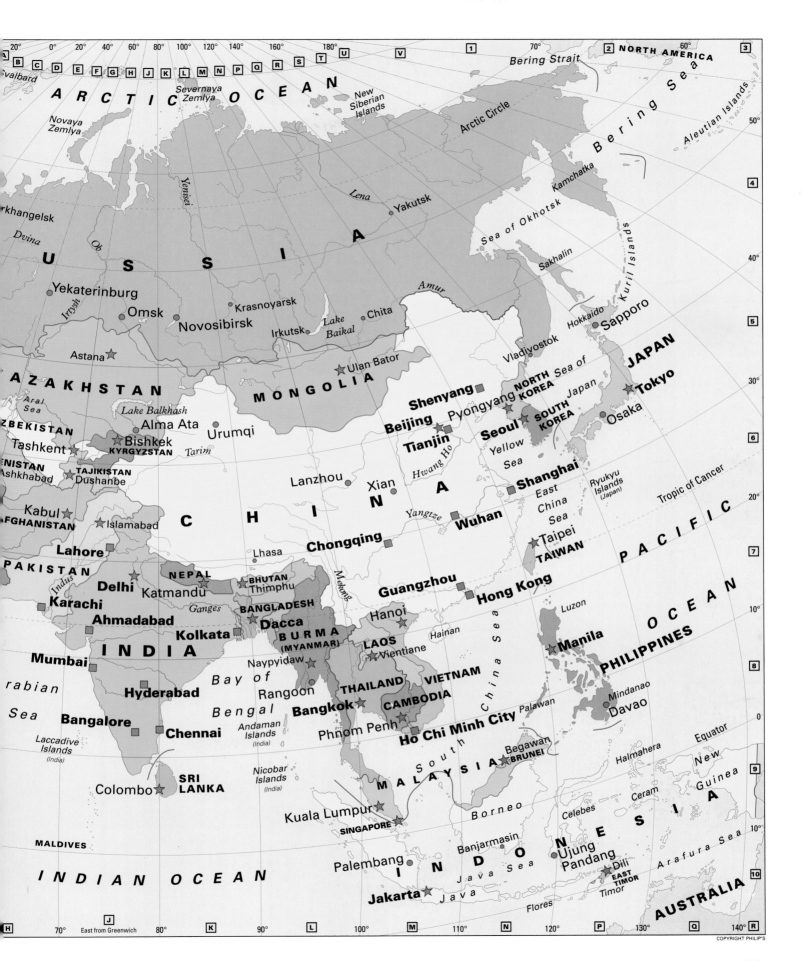

Africa

- *Africa is the second largest continent. Asia is the largest.*
- *There are over 50 countries, some of them small in area and population. The population of Africa is growing more quickly than any other continent.*
- *Parts of Africa have a dry, desert climate. Other parts are tropical.*

- *The highest mountains run from north to south on the eastern side of Africa. The Great Rift Valley is a volcanic valley that was formed 10 to 20 million years ago by a crack in the Earth's crust. Mount Kenya and Mount Kilimanjaro are examples of old volcanoes in the area.*
- *The Sahara desert is the largest desert in the world.*

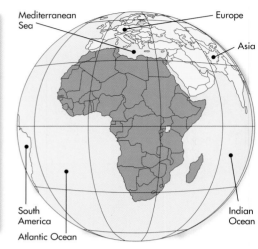

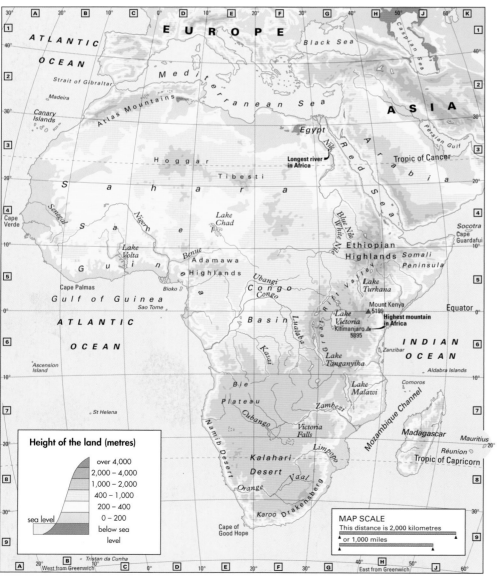

Largest countries – by area

(thousand square kilometres)

Sudan	2,506
Algeria	2,382
Congo (Dem. Rep.)	2,345
Libya	1,760
Chad	1,284
Niger	1,267

Largest countries – by population

(million people)

Nigeria	132
Egypt	79
Ethiopia	75
Congo (Dem. Rep.)	63
South Africa	44
Tanzania	37

Largest cities

(million people)

Cairo (EGYPT)	11.1
Lagos (NIGERIA)	11.1
Kinshasa (CONGO, DEM. REP.)	5.7
Alexandria (EGYPT)	3.8
Casablanca (MOROCCO)	3.7

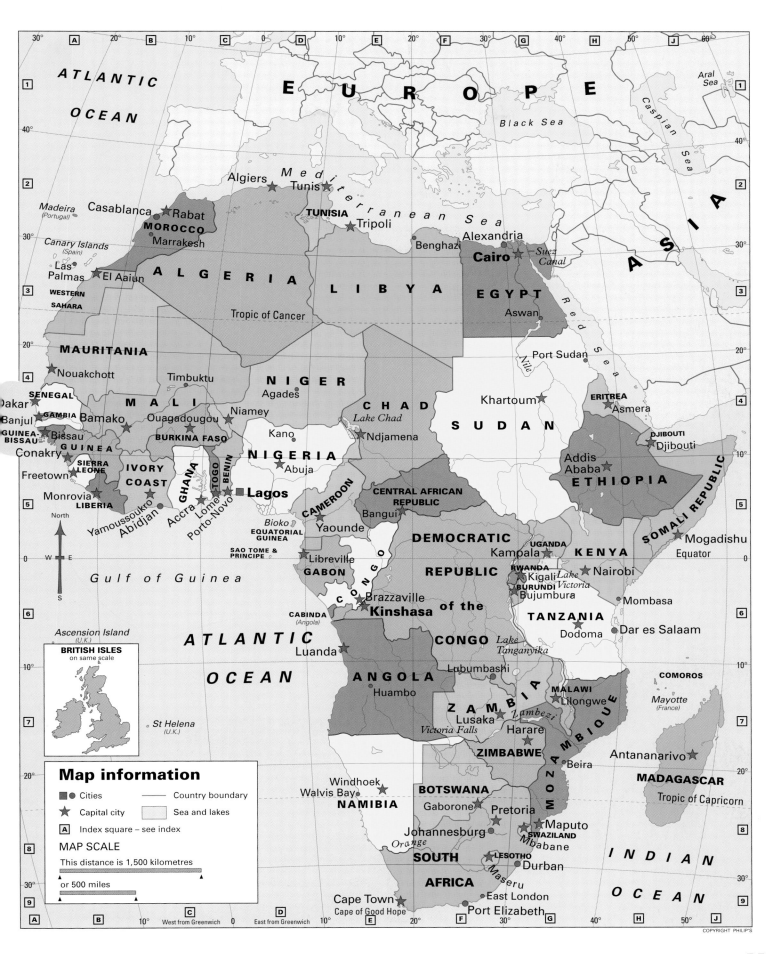

ATLANTIC
OCEAN

EUROPE

Black Sea

Aral Sea

Caspian Sea

ASIA

Mediterranean Sea

Algiers ★ Tunis
TUNISIA
Tripoli ★

Madeira (Portugal)
Casablanca ★ Rabat
MOROCCO
Marrakesh

Benghazi

Alexandria
Cairo ★
Suez Canal

Canary Islands (Spain)
Las Palmas
El Aaiun ★

ALGERIA

LIBYA

EGYPT

WESTERN
SAHARA

Tropic of Cancer

Aswan

Red Sea

MAURITANIA

NIGER

Khartoum ★

Port Sudan

ERITREA
Asmera ★

Nouakchott ★
SENEGAL
Dakar ★
GAMBIA
Banjul ★
GUINEA-BISSAU
Bissau ★
Conakry ★
GUINEA
SIERRA LEONE
Freetown ★
Monrovia ★
LIBERIA

Timbuktu

MALI
Bamako ★
Ouagadougou ★
BURKINA FASO

Agades

Niamey ★

Kano

Lake Chad

CHAD

Ndjamena ★

SUDAN

DJIBOUTI
Djibouti ★

Addis Ababa ★

ETHIOPIA

SOMALI REPUBLIC

IVORY COAST
Yamoussoukro ★
Abidjan

GHANA
Accra ★
TOGO
Lome ★
BENIN
Porto-Novo ★

NIGERIA
Abuja ★
Lagos ■

CAMEROON
Yaounde ★

Bioko
EQUATORIAL GUINEA

SAO TOME & PRINCIPE

CENTRAL AFRICAN REPUBLIC
Bangui ★

Libreville ★
GABON

CONGO

DEMOCRATIC

REPUBLIC

of the

CONGO

UGANDA
Kampala ★

KENYA
Nairobi ★

Mogadishu ★
Equator

RWANDA
Kigali ★
BURUNDI
Bujumbura ★
Lake Victoria

Mombasa

North
W — E
S

Gulf of Guinea

Brazzaville ★
Kinshasa ★

CABINDA (Angola)

ATLANTIC

OCEAN

Luanda ★

ANGOLA

Huambo

Lake Tanganyika

TANZANIA
Dodoma ★
Dar es Salaam

Ascension Island (U.K.)

BRITISH ISLES
on same scale

St Helena (U.K.)

Lubumbashi

ZAMBIA
Lusaka ★

Zambezi

Victoria Falls

MALAWI
Lilongwe ★

COMOROS

Mayotte (France)

Harare ★
ZIMBABWE

Beira

MOZAMBIQUE

Antananarivo ★

MADAGASCAR

Tropic of Capricorn

Windhoek ★
Walvis Bay

NAMIBIA

BOTSWANA
Gaborone ★

Pretoria ★

Johannesburg
Orange

SOUTH

AFRICA

Maputo ★
SWAZILAND
Mbabane ★

LESOTHO
Maseru ★
Durban

East London

INDIAN

OCEAN

Cape Town ★
Cape of Good Hope

Port Elizabeth

Map information

■ ● Cities	—	Country boundary
★ Capital city		Sea and lakes
Ａ Index square – see index		

MAP SCALE

This distance is 1,500 kilometres

or 500 miles

West from Greenwich   East from Greenwich

COPYRIGHT PHILIP'S

55

Australia and Oceania

- The continent is often called Oceania. It is made up of the huge island of Australia and thousands of other islands in the Pacific Ocean.
- It is the smallest continent, only about a sixth the size of Asia.
- The highest mountain is on the Indonesian part of New Guinea which many consider to be part of Asia.

Largest countries – by area

(thousand square kilometres)	
Australia	7,741
Papua New Guinea	463
New Zealand	271

Largest countries – by population

(million people)	
Australia	20
Papua New Guinea	6

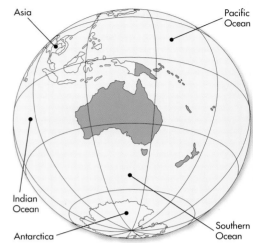

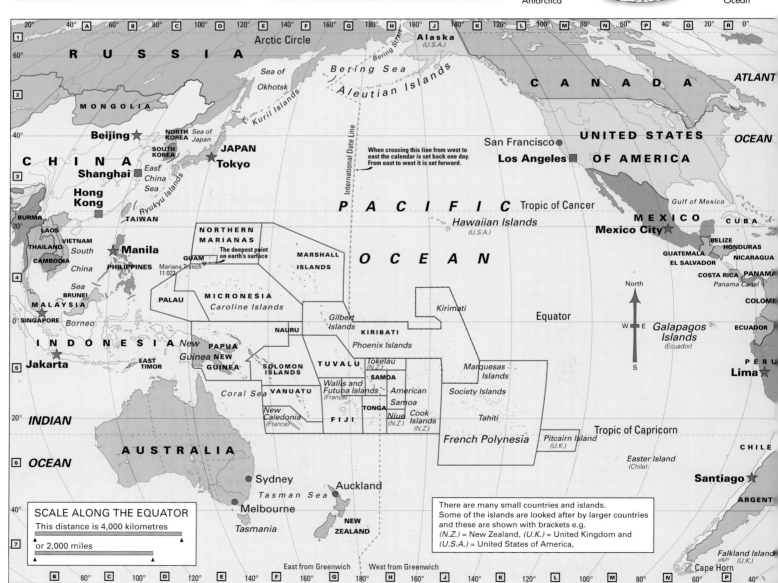

When crossing this line from west to east the calendar is set back one day. From east to west it is set forward.

The deepest point on earth's surface
Mariana Trench
11 022

SCALE ALONG THE EQUATOR
This distance is 4,000 kilometres
or 2,000 miles

There are many small countries and islands.
Some of the islands are looked after by larger countries and these are shown with brackets e.g.
(N.Z.) = New Zealand, (U.K.) = United Kingdom and
(U.S.A.) = United States of America,

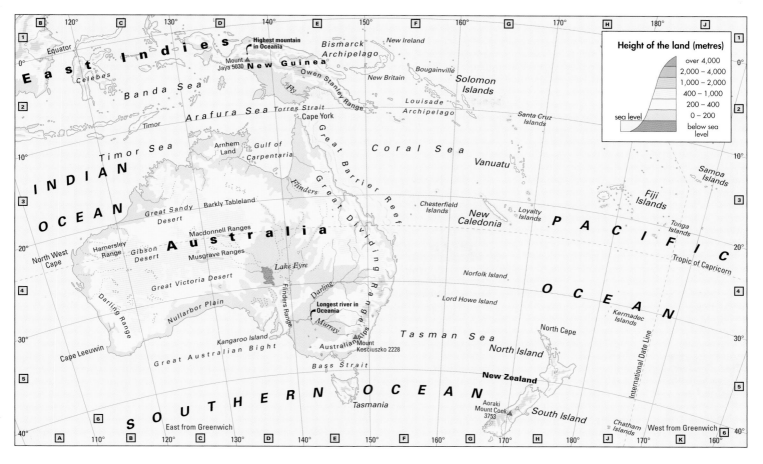

Height of the land (metres)

- over 4,000
- 2,000 – 4,000
- 1,000 – 2,000
- 400 – 1,000
- 200 – 400
- 0 – 200
- below sea level

sea level

Top map labels:

East Indies · Equator · Celebes · Banda Sea · Timor · Arafura Sea · Torres Strait · Cape York · New Guinea · Highest mountain in Oceania · Mount Jaya 5030 · Owen Stanley Range · Fly · Bismarck Archipelago · New Ireland · New Britain · Bougainville · Solomon Islands · Louisade Archipelago · Santa Cruz Islands · Coral Sea · Vanuatu · Samoa Islands · Fiji Islands · Tonga Islands

INDIAN OCEAN · Timor Sea · Arnhem Land · Gulf of Carpentaria · Great Barrier Reef · Chesterfield Islands · New Caledonia · Loyalty Islands · PACIFIC OCEAN

Great Sandy Desert · Barkly Tableland · Macdonnell Ranges · Australia · Hamersley Range · Gibson Desert · Musgrave Ranges · Lake Eyre · Norfolk Island · Tropic of Capricorn

North West Cape · Great Victoria Desert · Darling · Lord Howe Island · Kermadec Islands

Darling Range · Nullarbor Plain · Flinders Range · Longest river in Oceania · Murray · Tasman Sea · North Cape · North Island

Cape Leeuwin · Kangaroo Island · Great Australian Bight · Australian Alps · Mount Kosciuszko 2228 · New Zealand · Aoraki Mount Cook 3753 · South Island · International Date Line

Bass Strait · Tasmania · Chatham Islands

SOUTHERN OCEAN · East from Greenwich · West from Greenwich

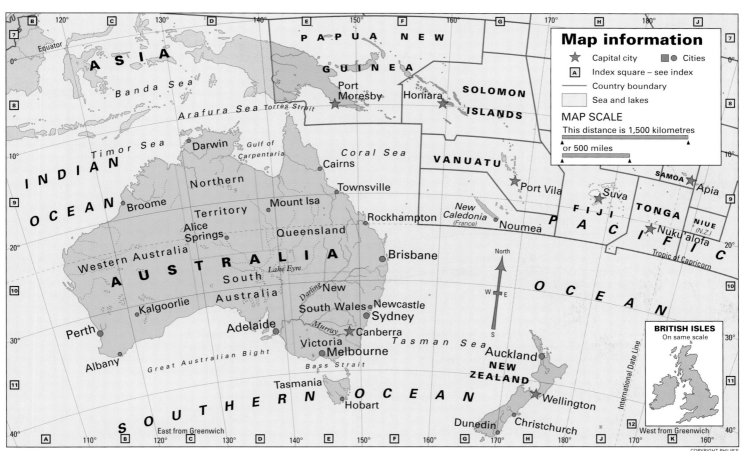

Map information

- ★ Capital city
- ● Cities
- Ⓐ Index square – see index
- —— Country boundary
- Sea and lakes

MAP SCALE

This distance is 1,500 kilometres

or 500 miles

Bottom map labels:

ASIA · Equator · Banda Sea · Arafura Sea · Torres Strait · PAPUA NEW GUINEA · Port Moresby · Honiara · SOLOMON ISLANDS

INDIAN OCEAN · Timor Sea · Darwin · Gulf of Carpentaria · Coral Sea · Cairns · Townsville · VANUATU · Port Vila · Suva · SAMOA · Apia

Broome · Northern Territory · Mount Isa · Rockhampton · New Caledonia (France) · Noumea · FIJI · TONGA · NIUE (N.Z.) · Nuku'alofa

Alice Springs · Queensland · Brisbane · PACIFIC OCEAN · Tropic of Capricorn

Western Australia · AUSTRALIA · Lake Eyre · South · New · North

Kalgoorlie · Australia · Darling · South Wales · Newcastle · Sydney

Perth · Adelaide · Murray · Canberra · Tasman Sea · Auckland

Albany · Great Australian Bight · Victoria · Melbourne · NEW ZEALAND · Wellington

Tasmania · Hobart · SOUTHERN OCEAN · Dunedin · Christchurch

East from Greenwich · West from Greenwich · International Date Line

BRITISH ISLES
On same scale

COPYRIGHT PHILIP'S

North America

- North America is the third largest continent. It is half the size of Asia. It stretches almost from the Equator to the North Pole.
- Three countries – Canada, the United States and Mexico – make up most of the continent.
- Greenland, the largest island in the world, is included within North America.

- In the east there are a series of large lakes. These are called the Great Lakes. A large waterfall called Niagara Falls is between Lake Erie and Lake Ontario. The St Lawrence river connects the Great Lakes with the Atlantic Ocean.
- North and South America are joined by a narrow strip of land called the Isthmus of Panama.

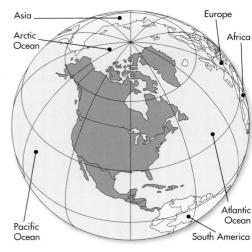

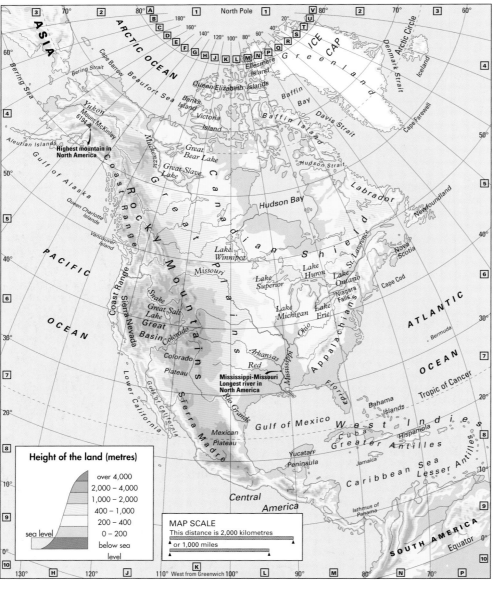

Largest countries – by area

(thousand square kilometres)

Canada	9,971
United States	9,629
Greenland	2,176
Mexico	1,958
Nicaragua	130
Honduras	112

Largest countries – by population

(million people)

United States	301
Mexico	107
Canada	33
Guatemala	12
Cuba	11
Dominican Republic	9

Largest cities

(million people)

Mexico City (MEXICO)	19.0
New York (USA)	17.8
Los Angeles (USA)	11.8
Chicago (USA)	8.3
Philadelphia (USA)	5.1

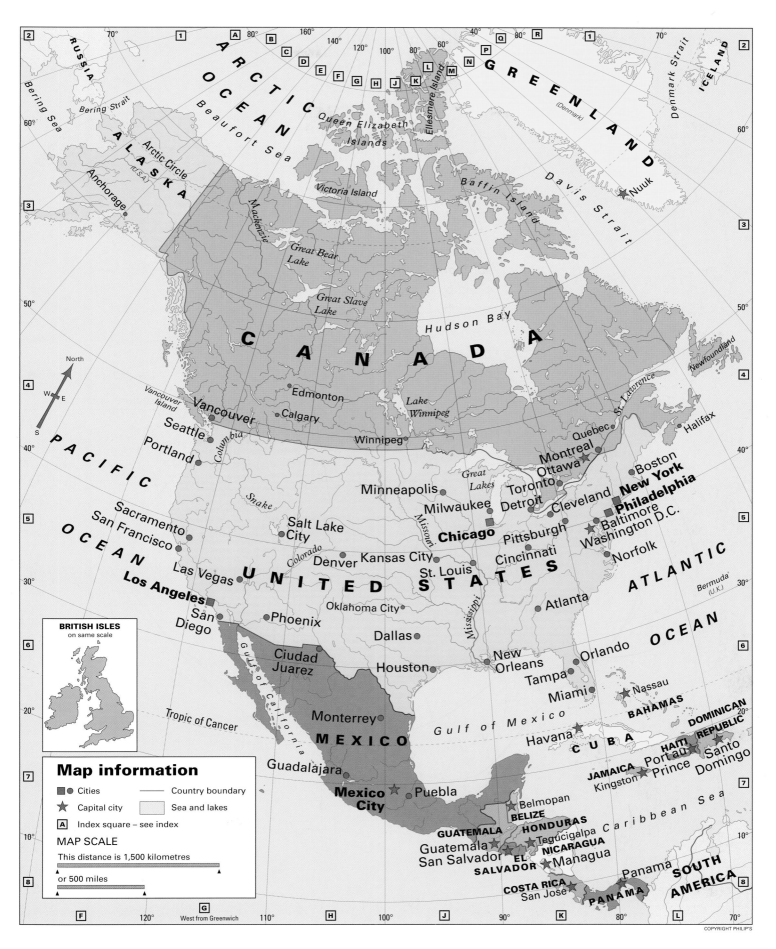

RUSSIA
ALASKA (USA)
Anchorage

ARCTIC OCEAN

Bering Sea
Bering Strait
Beaufort Sea
Arctic Circle

GREENLAND (Denmark)
ICELAND
Denmark Strait
Nuuk
Davis Strait

Queen Elizabeth Islands
Ellesmere Island
Baffin Island

Mackenzie
Victoria Island
Great Bear Lake
Great Slave Lake

CANADA

Hudson Bay

Newfoundland

North
W E
S

Vancouver Island
Vancouver
Seattle
Portland
Columbia

Edmonton
Calgary
Lake Winnipeg
Winnipeg

Quebec
Montreal
Ottawa
Toronto
St. Lawrence
Halifax

PACIFIC OCEAN

Sacramento
San Francisco
Las Vegas
Los Angeles
San Diego

Snake
Salt Lake City
Colorado
Denver

UNITED STATES
Minneapolis
Milwaukee
Great Lakes
Detroit
Chicago
Missouri
Kansas City
St. Louis
Pittsburgh
Cincinnati

Cleveland
New York
Philadelphia
Baltimore
Washington D.C.
Norfolk
Boston

ATLANTIC
Bermuda (U.K.)

Phoenix
Oklahoma City
Dallas
Mississippi
Atlanta

BRITISH ISLES
on same scale

Ciudad Juarez
Houston
New Orleans
Tampa
Miami
Orlando
OCEAN

Gulf of California
Tropic of Cancer
Monterrey

MEXICO
Guadalajara

Gulf of Mexico
Havana
CUBA
Nassau
BAHAMAS

HAITI
DOMINICAN REPUBLIC
JAMAICA
Kingston
Port au Prince
Santo Domingo

Mexico City
Puebla

Belmopan
BELIZE
GUATEMALA
Guatemala
San Salvador
EL SALVADOR
HONDURAS
Tegucigalpa
NICARAGUA
Managua

Caribbean Sea

COSTA RICA
San Jose
PANAMA
Panama
SOUTH AMERICA

Map information

- Cities
- ⭐ Capital city
- A Index square – see index
- —— Country boundary
- Sea and lakes

MAP SCALE

This distance is 1,500 kilometres

or 500 miles

COPYRIGHT PHILIP'S

59

South America

- The Amazon is the second longest river in the world. The Nile is the longest river, but more water flows from the Amazon into the ocean than from any other river.
- The range of mountains called the Andes runs for over 7,500 km from north to south on the western side of the continent. There are many volcanoes in the Andes.

- Lake Titicaca is the largest lake in the continent. It has an area of 8,300 sq km and is 3,800 metres above sea level.
- Spanish and Portuguese are the principal languages spoken in South America.
- Brazil is the largest country in area and population and is the richest in the continent.

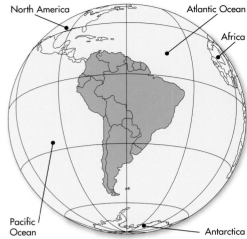

Largest countries – by area

(thousand square kilometres)	
Brazil	8,514
Argentina	2,780
Peru	1,285
Colombia	1,139
Bolivia	1,099
Venezuela	912

Largest countries – by population

(million people)	
Brazil	188
Colombia	44
Argentina	40
Peru	28
Venezuela	26
Chile	16

Largest cities

(million people)	
Sao Paulo (BRAZIL)	18.0
Buenos Aires (ARGENTINA)	13.3
Rio de Janeiro (BRAZIL)	11.5
Lima (PERU)	8.2
Bogota (COLOMBIA)	7.6

Map labels

Cuba, Jamaica, Hispaniola, Greater Antilles, Lesser Antilles, Caribbean Sea, ATLANTIC OCEAN, Central America, Galapagos Islands, Point Parinas, Magdalena, Llanos, Orinoco, Guiana Highlands, Negro, Amazon Basin, Amazon, Selvas, Ucayali, Madeira, Tapajos, Tocantins, Longest river in South America, Equator, Cape Sao Roque, Sao Francisco, Plateau of Mato Grosso, Brazilian Highlands, Lake Titicaca, Gran Chaco, Paraguay, Parana, Cape Frio, Tropic of Capricorn, PACIFIC OCEAN, Highest mountain in South America, Mount Aconcagua 6962, Pampas, Rio de la Plata, ATLANTIC OCEAN, Patagonia, Falkland Islands, Cape Horn, Andes

Height of the land (metres)

- over 4,000
- 2,000 – 4,000
- 1,000 – 2,000
- 400 – 1,000
- 200 – 400
- 0 – 200
- sea level
- below sea level

MAP SCALE
This distance is 2,000 kilometres
or 1,000 miles

West from Greenwich

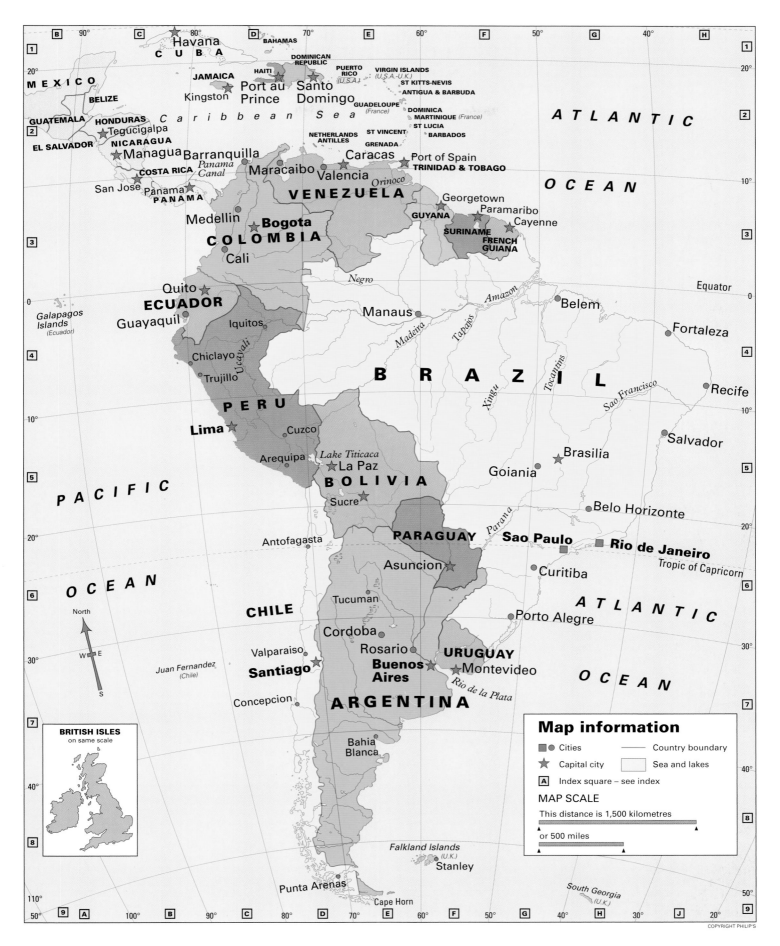

B 90° C 80° BAHAMAS D 70° E 60° F 50° G 40° H

1
Havana
C U B A
MEXICO 20°
JAMAICA HAITI DOMINICAN REPUBLIC PUERTO RICO (U.S.A.) VIRGIN ISLANDS (U.S.A.-U.K.)
BELIZE Kingston Port au Santo ST KITTS-NEVIS
GUATEMALA HONDURAS Prince Domingo GUADELOUPE (France) ANTIGUA & BARBUDA A T L A N T I C **2**
Tegucigalpa Caribbean Sea DOMINICA MARTINIQUE (France)
EL SALVADOR NICARAGUA ST VINCENT ST LUCIA O C E A N
Managua Barranquilla NETHERLANDS BARBADOS
COSTA RICA Panama Caracas ANTILLES GRENADA
San Jose Canal Maracaibo Port of Spain **3**
Panama Valencia TRINIDAD & TOBAGO
PANAMA VENEZUELA Orinoco
Medellin Georgetown Paramaribo
Bogota GUYANA Cayenne
COLOMBIA SURINAME FRENCH
Cali GUIANA

Negro Equator **0**
Quito Amazon
ECUADOR Belem
Galapagos Guayaquil Manaus Fortaleza **4**
Islands Iquitos Madeira Tapajos
(Ecuador) Chiclayo Xingu Tocantins
Trujillo Ucayali Recife
PERU Sao Francisco **5**
Lima Salvador
Cuzco
Arequipa Brasilia
Lake Titicaca Goiania
La Paz
BOLIVIA Belo Horizonte **5**
Sucre
PACIFIC Parana
Antofagasta PARAGUAY Sao Paulo Rio de Janeiro **20°**
Asuncion Tropic of Capricorn
O C E A N Curitiba **6**
CHILE Tucuman ATLANTIC
Porto Alegre
Cordoba URUGUAY
Valparaiso Rosario Montevideo O C E A N **30°**
Santiago Buenos
Juan Fernandez Aires Rio de la Plata **7**
(Chile) ARGENTINA
Concepcion

Bahia
Blanca
BRITISH ISLES
on same scale

Map information
Cities Country boundary
Capital city Sea and lakes
Falkland Islands A Index square – see index
(U.K.)
Stanley MAP SCALE
This distance is 1,500 kilometres
Punta Arenas
Cape Horn or 500 miles
South Georgia
(U.K.)
COPYRIGHT PHILIP'S

61

Polar Regions

The Polar Regions are the areas around the North Pole and the South Pole. The area around the North Pole is called the **Arctic** and the area around the South Pole is called the **Antarctic**. The sun never shines straight down on the Arctic or Antarctic so they are very cold – the coldest places on Earth. The Arctic consists of frozen water. Some parts of Northern Europe, North America and Asia are inside the Arctic Circle. A group of people called the Inuit live there.

Map information

- Cities and towns
- ★ Capital cities
- ⊙ (Japan) Scientific stations in the Antarctic
- Land covered in ice
- Sea covered in ice
- Ice sometimes in the sea

MAP SCALE
This distance is 1,500 kilometres
or 500 miles

The Antarctic is a continent. It is bigger than Europe or Australia and has no permanent population. Most of the land consists of ice which is thousands of metres thick. At the edges, chunks of ice break off to make icebergs. These float out to sea. The diagram below shows a cross-section through Antarctica between two of the scientific research stations, Siple and Casey. It shows how thick the ice is on the ice sheets.

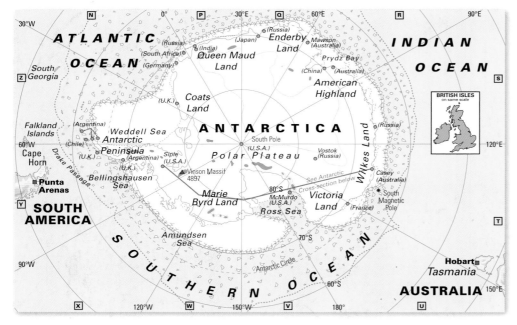

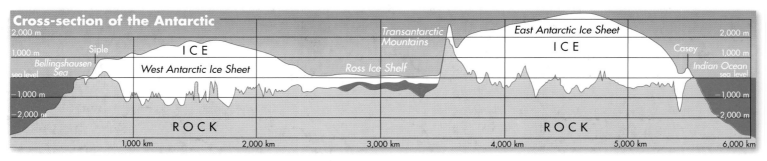

Cross-section of the Antarctic

UK, Europe and the World

United Nations

The UN is the largest international organization in the world. The headquarters are in New York and 192 countries are members. It was formed in 1945 to help solve world problems and to help keep world peace. The UN sends peacekeeping forces to areas where there are problems.

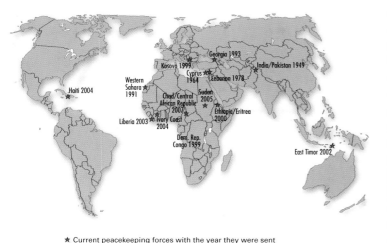

★ Current peacekeeping forces with the year they were sent

Population (million people)

Country	Population
Austria	8
Belgium	10
Bulgaria	7
Cyprus	0.8
Czech Republic	10
Denmark	5
Estonia	1
Finland	5
France	61
Germany	82
Greece	11
Hungary	10
Ireland	4
Italy	58
Latvia	2
Lithuania	4
Luxembourg	0.5
Malta	0.4
Netherlands	16
Poland	39
Portugal	11
Romania	22
Slovak Republic	5
Slovenia	2
Spain	40
Sweden	9
UK	61

European Union

☐ EU member countries

The EU was first formed in 1951. Six countries were members. Now there are 27 countries in the EU. These countries meet to discuss agriculture, industry and trade as well as social and political issues. The headquarters are in Brussels. Cyprus, the Czech Republic, Estonia, Hungary, Latvia, Lithuania, Malta, Poland, the Slovak Republic and Slovenia joined the EU in 2004. Bulgaria and Romania joined in 2007.

The Commonwealth

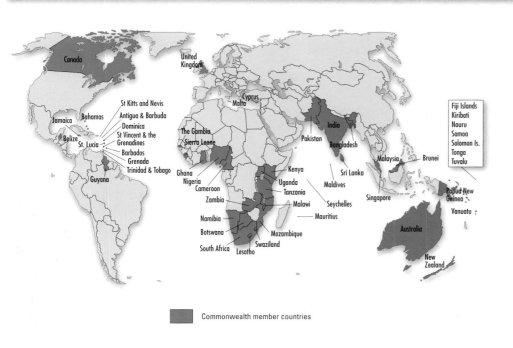

Commonwealth member countries

The Commonwealth is a group of 53 independent countries which used to belong to the British Empire. It is organized by a group of people called the Secretariat which is based in London. Queen Elizabeth II is the head of the Commonwealth. About every two years the heads of the different governments meet to discuss world problems. These meetings are held in different countries in the Commonwealth.

Index

The names in the index are in alphabetical order. To find a place on a map in the atlas, first find the name in the index. The first number after the place name is the page number. After the page number there is a letter and another number. The **letter** shows you the **column** where the place is on the map and the **number** shows you the **row**. If the place name goes across more than one square, the reference is to the square where the name begins.

Place	Pg	Ref	Place	Pg	Ref	Place	Pg	Ref	Place	Pg	Ref	Place	Pg	Ref	Place	Pg	Ref
Ivory Coast	55	C5	Luanda	55	D6	Ness, Loch	26	D2	Plymouth	25	B7	Sligo	27	C2	Tokyo	53	R5
Jakarta	53	M9	Lurgan	27	E2	Netherlands	51	H5	Podgorica	51	L7	Slough	25	F6	Tonga	57	J9
Jamaica	59	K7	Lusaka	55	F7	New Guinea	57	D2	Poland	51	L5	Slovak Republic	51	L6	Toronto	59	K4
Japan	53	R5	Luton	25	F6	New Orleans	59	K5	Poole	25	D7	Slovenia	51	K6	Torquay	25	C7
Japan, Sea of	53	Q4	Luxembourg	51	J6	New York	59	L4	Port Laoise	27	D3	Snaefell	24	B3	Tralee	27	B4
Java	53	M9	Lvov	51	M6	New Zealand	57	G11	Port Moresby	57	E8	Snowdon	24	B4	Trent, River	24	F4
Jersey	25	D8	Lyons	51	H6	Newbury	25	E6	Port of Spain	61	E2	Sofia	51	M7	Trinidad & Tobago	61	E2
Jerusalem	52	D5	Macedonia	51	M7	Newcastle-under-Lyme	24	D4	Port Talbot	25	C6	Solihull	25	E5	Tripoli	55	E2
John o'Groats	26	E1	Madagascar	55	H8	Newcastle-upon-Tyne	24	E2	Portadown	27	E2	Solomon Islands	57	G8	Tunis	55	D2
Jordan	52	E6	Madrid	50	G8	Newfoundland	59	N4	Port-au-Prince	59	L7	Somali Republic	55	H5	Tunisia	55	D2
Jura	26	C4	Maidstone	25	G6	Newhaven	25	G7	Portland Bill	25	D7	South Africa	55	F8	Turin	51	J7
Kabul	53	H5	Majorca	50	H8	Newport	25	D6	Porto-Novo	55	C5	South America	30	C5	Turkey	52	D5
Kampala	55	F5	Malawi	55	G7	Newquay	25	A7	Portsmouth	25	E7	South China Sea	53	M8	Turkmenistan	52	G5
Karachi	53	H6	Malaysia	53	M8	Newry	27	E2	Portugal	50	F8	South Downs	25	F7	Tuvalu	56	G5
Katmandu	53	J6	Maldives	53	H8	Niagara Falls	58	N5	Prague	51	L6	South Korea	53	P5	Tweed, River	26	F4
Kazakhstan	53	G4	Mali	55	C4	Niamey	55	D4	Preston	24	D4	South Pole	62	S	Tyne, River	24	E3
Kenya	55	G5	Malin Head	27	D1	Nicaragua	59	K7	Pretoria	55	F8	Southampton	25	E7	Tynemouth	24	E2
Khartoum	55	F4	Mallaig	26	C3	Nicosia	51	P8	Pristina	51	M7	Southend	25	G6	Uganda	55	G5
Kiev	51	N5	Malta	51	K8	Niger	55	D4	Pyongyang	53	N4	Southern Ocean	31	K7	Ukraine	51	M6
Kigali	55	G6	Man, Isle of	24	B3	Niger, River	54	D4	Pyrenees	50	G7	Southern Uplands	26	D4	Ulan Bator	53	M4
Kilimanjaro, Mount	54	G6	Managua	59	K7	Nigeria	55	D4	Qatar	52	F6	Spain	50	F7	Ullapool	26	C2
Kilkenny	27	D4	Manchester	24	D4	Nile, River	54	G3	Quebec	59	L4	Spey, River	26	E2	Ulster	27	D2
Killarney	27	B4	Manila	53	P7	North America	30	C2	Quito	61	C4	Sri Lanka	53	K8	United Arab Emirates	52	F6
Kilmarnock	26	D4	Mansfield	24	E4	North Channel	27	F1	Rabat	55	C2	St Albans	25	F6	United Kingdom	50	G4
King's Lynn	24	G5	Maputo	55	G8	North Downs	25	F6	Rangoon	53	L7	St Andrews	26	F3	United States	59	G5
Kingston	59	K7	Margate	25	H6	North Korea	53	P4	Reading	25	E6	St George's Channel	27	E5	Ural Mountains	50	V2
Kingston upon Hull	24	F4	Marrakesh	55	C2	North Pole	62	E	Red Sea	55	G3	St Lucia	61	E2	Uruguay	61	F7
Kinshasa	55	E6	Marseilles	51	J7	North Sea	51	H4	Ree, Lough	27	D3	St Petersburg	51	P4	Uzbekistan	53	G4
Kintyre	26	C4	Maseru	55	F9	North West Highlands	26	C2	Reigate	25	F6	Stafford	24	D5	Valletta	51	K8
Kiribati	56	H5	Mask, Lough	27	B3	North York Moors	24	E3	Réunion	54	J8	Stansted Airport	25	G6	Vancouver	59	F3
Kirkcaldy	26	E3	Mauritania	55	B4	Northampton	25	F5	Reykjavik	50	C3	Stevenage	25	F6	Vanuatu	57	F9
Kirkwall	26	F6	Mauritius	54	J7	Northern Ireland	27	D2	Rhine, River	51	J6	Stirling	26	E3	Venezuela	61	D3
Knockmealdown Mountains	27	C4	Mbabane	55	G8	Norway	51	J3	Rhondda	25	C6	Stockholm	51	K4	Verde, Cape	54	B4
Kolkata	53	K6	McKinley, Mount	58	E3	Norwich	24	H5	Rhone, River	51	J7	Stockport	24	D4	Victoria Falls	54	F7
Kosovo	51	M7	Mecca	52	F6	Nottingham	24	E5	Ribble, River	24	D4	Stockton	24	E3	Victoria, Lake	54	G6
Kuala Lumpur	53	L8	Mediterranean Sea	50	H8	Nouakchott	55	B4	Riga	51	N4	Stoke on Trent	24	D4	Vienna	51	K6
Kuwait	52	F6	Mekong, River	53	M6	Nuneaton	25	E5	Rio de Janeiro	61	G6	Stonehenge	25	E6	Vientiane	53	M7
Kyle of Lochalsh	26	C2	Melbourne	57	E11	Nuuk	59	P2	Riyadh	52	F6	Stornoway	26	B1	Vietnam	53	M7
Kyrgyzstan	53	J4	Merthyr Tydfil	25	C6	Oban	26	C3	Rocky Mountains	58	H4	Strabane	27	D2	Vilnius	51	N5
La Paz	61	E5	Mexico	59	H6	Oceania	31	S5	Romania	51	M6	Stranraer	26	C4	Vladivostock	53	P4
Lagos	55	D5	Mexico City	59	H7	Oldham	24	D4	Rome	51	K7	Stratford-upon-Avon	25	E5	Volga, River	51	S6
Lahore	53	H5	Mexico, Gulf of	59	J6	Omagh	27	D2	Roscommon	27	C3	Sucre	61	E5	Wales	25	C5
Lake District	24	C3	Miami	59	K6	Oman	52	G6	Ross Sea	62	V	Sudan	55	F4	Walsall	25	E5
Lancaster	24	D3	Michigan, Lake	58	L5	Ontario, Lake	58	N5	Rosslare	27	E4	Suez Canal	55	G2	Warrington	24	D4
Land's End	25	A7	Middlesbrough	24	E3	Oporto	50	E7	Rotherham	24	E4	Sunderland	24	E3	Warsaw	51	L5
Laos	53	L7	Milan	51	J6	Orange, River	54	E8	Rugby	25	E5	Superior, Lake	58	L5	Wash, The	24	G5
Lapland	50	M2	Milford Haven	25	A6	Orinoco, River	60	E3	Russia	52	F2	Suriname	61	F3	Washington D.C.	59	L5
Larne	27	F2	Milton Keynes	25	F5	Orkney Islands	26	E7	Rwanda	55	F6	Swansea	25	C6	Waterford	27	D4
Latvia	51	M4	Minsk	51	N5	Orlando	59	K6	Sahara, desert	54	B4	Swaziland	55	G8	Watford	25	F6
Lebanon	52	E5	Mississippi, River	59	J5	Osaka	53	Q5	Sakhalin	53	R3	Sweden	51	K4	Wellington	57	H12
Leeds	24	E4	Missouri, River	59	J4	Oslo	51	J3	Salisbury	25	E6	Swindon	25	E6	West Bromwich	25	D5
Leicester	25	E5	Mogadishu	55	H5	Ottawa	59	K4	Salisbury Plain	25	D6	Switzerland	51	J6	Western Sahara	55	B3
Leinster	27	D3	Moldova	51	N6	Ouagadougou	55	C4	Samoa	57	J9	Sydney	57	F11	Weston-super-Mare	25	D6
Lerwick	26	J8	Monaco	51	J7	Ouse, River	24	E4	San Francisco	59	E5	Syria	52	E5	Westport	27	B3
Lesotho	55	F8	Monaghan	27	D2	Outer Hebrides	26	A2	San Jose	59	K8	Taipei	53	P6	Wexford	27	E4
Letterkenny	27	D2	Mongolia	53	L4	Ox Mountains	27	C2	San Marino	51	K7	Taiwan	53	P6	Weymouth	25	D7
Lewis	26	B1	Monrovia	55	B5	Oxford	25	E6	San Salvador	59	J7	Tajikistan	53	H5	Wick	26	E1
Liberia	55	B5	Montenegro	51	L7	Pacific Ocean	30	B4	Sana	52	F7	Tallinn	51	N4	Wicklow	27	E4
Libreville	55	E6	Montevideo	61	F7	Paisley	26	D4	Santiago	61	D7	Tanganyika, Lake	54	F6	Wicklow Mountains	27	E4
Libya	55	E3	Montreal	59	K4	Pakistan	53	H6	Santo Domingo	59	L7	Tanzania	55	G6	Wight, Isle of	25	E7
Liffey, River	27	E3	Montrose	26	F3	Panama	59	K8	Sao Paulo	61	F6	Tashkent	53	H4	Winchester	25	E6
Lilongwe	55	G7	Moray Firth	26	E2	Panama Canal	61	D2	Sarajevo	51	L7	Tasmania	57	D12	Windhoek	55	E8
Lima	61	C5	Morecambe Bay	24	C3	Papua New Guinea	57	E8	Sardinia	51	J7	Taunton	25	C6	Winnipeg	59	H4
Limerick	27	C4	Morocco	55	C2	Paraguay	61	E6	Saudi Arabia	52	F6	Tay, River	26	E3	Wolverhampton	25	D5
Lincoln	24	F4	Moscow	51	Q4	Paramaribo	61	F3	Scafell Pike	24	C3	Tbilisi	52	F4	Worcester	25	D5
Lincolnshire Wolds	24	F4	Mourne Mountains	27	E2	Paris	51	H6	Scarborough	24	F3	Tees, River	24	E3	Worthing	25	F7
Lisbon	50	F8	Mozambique	55	G8	Pembroke	25	B6	Scilly Isles	25	A8	Tegucigalpa	59	K7	Wrath, Cape	26	C1
Lisburn	27	E2	Mull	26	C3	Pennines	24	D3	Scotland	26	D3	Tehran	52	G5	Wuhan	53	N6
Lithuania	51	M4	Mullingar	27	D3	Penzance	25	A7	Seattle	59	F4	Telford	24	D5	Wye, River	25	C5
Liverpool	24	C4	Mumbai	53	H7	Perth	26	E3	Senegal	55	B4	Thailand	53	L7	Yamoussoukro	55	B5
Lizard Point	25	A8	Munich	51	J6	Peru	61	D5	Seoul	53	P5	Thames, River	25	G6	Yangtze, River	53	M5
Ljubljana	51	K6	Munster	27	B4	Peterborough	25	F5	Serbia	51	L7	The Hague	51	J5	Yaounde	55	E5
Llandudno	24	C4	Muscat	52	G6	Peterhead	26	G2	Severn, River	25	D6	Thimphu	53	L6	Yellow Sea	53	P5
Llanelli	25	B6	Nairobi	55	G6	Philadelphia	59	L4	Shanghai	53	P5	Thurso	26	E1	Yemen	52	F7
Lome	55	C5	Namibia	55	E8	Philippines	53	P7	Shannon, River	27	C3	Tibet, Plateau of	52	K5	Yerevan	52	E4
Lomond, Loch	26	D3	Naypyidaw	53	L7	Phnom Penh	53	L7	Sheffield	24	E4	Tigris, River	52	F5	York	24	E4
London	25	G6	Ndjamena	55	E4				Shetland Islands	26	J8	Timbuktu	55	C4	Yorkshire Wolds	24	F4
Londonderry	27	D2	Neagh, Lough	27	E2				Shrewsbury	24	D5	Tipperary	27	C4	Zagreb	51	L6
Los Angeles	59	F5	Neath	25	C6				Sierra Leone	55	B5	Tirane	51	M7	Zambezi, River	54	G7
Lowestoft	25	H5	Nenagh	27	C4				Singapore	53	L8	Titicaca, Lake	60	E5	Zambia	55	F7
			Nene, River	24	G5				Skopje	51	M7	Togo	55	D5	Zimbabwe	55	F7
			Nepal	53	K6				Skye	26	B2						